CW00551774

Chinese
Painting
Techniques

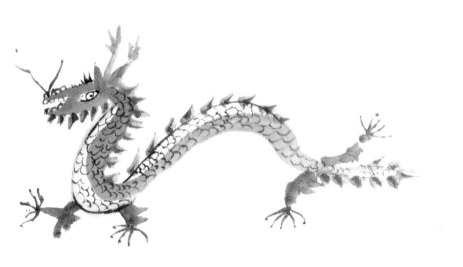

荷

珍朗

一千九百七十九年

璞龍

Chinese
Painting Techniques

A Complete Course

Jean Long

STUDIO
VISTA

Studio Vista
an imprint of
Cassell
Villiers House, 41/47 Strand
London WC2N 5JE

Copyright © Jean Long 1979, 1984, 1989
This compilation copyright © Cassell 1994

First published 1994

British Library Cataloguing in Publication Data
A catalogue record for this book is available from the British Library

ISBN 0 289 80114 1

This book has been compiled from Jean Long's *Chinese Ink Painting* (1984),
How to Paint the Chinese Way (1979) and *Practical Chinese Painting* (1989),
all previously published by Blandford Press.

Printed and bound in Portugal
by Printer Portuguesa

Typeset by Litho Link Ltd, Welshpool, Powys, Wales

Contents

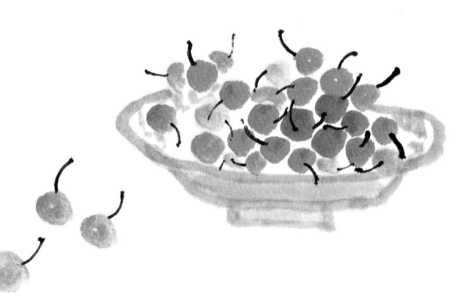

花魁

一千九百七十九年

Chinese Ink Painting and Calligraphy

Chinese Painting Equipment

The Four Treasures of the Studio

The brush, the ink stick, the ink stone and the paper – the implements needed for Chinese traditional painting and writing – have been known as the 'four treasures of the studio' since the end of the tenth century when there was a shop of that name selling the equipment in Anhui province.

These 'treasures' are the basic necessities required to paint traditional Chinese subjects in 'shades of black'.

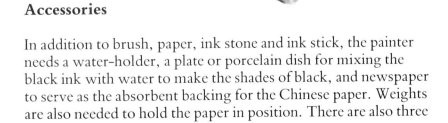

Accessories

In addition to brush, paper, ink stone and ink stick, the painter needs a water-holder, a plate or porcelain dish for mixing the black ink with water to make the shades of black, and newspaper to serve as the absorbent backing for the Chinese paper. Weights are also needed to hold the paper in position. There are also three special items included here: a wooden 'mountain' brush rest, an antique water dropper in the shape of a bird on a tree trunk, and a lotus leaf brush-washer. (Those shown are from the collection of P. Cherrett.)

Chinese Painting Brushes

All derive from the writing brush, but early writing was done with a whittled, sharpened willow stick on strips of bamboo. General Meng Tian who lived in the Ch'in Dynasty (221-207 BC) is credited with the invention of the brush of hair. In the story relating to this, it is said that as he was supervising the construction of the Great Wall he saw a tuft of goat's hair stuck to one of the stones, noticed its resemblance to the willow stick and tried to write with it.

The brush most used at present is a blend of the hairs of the weasel and the hare, but rabbit hair brushes, goat hair brushes, or even those made with panda hair or mouse whiskers are still available.

Much care is needed in the making of a brush. For instance, a brush of rabbit hair requires hair which is neither too soft nor too thick and has, therefore, to be obtained in the autumn when all the correct conditions are satisfied. The Chinese believe that every painter should possess his own brushes which, after training, take on his own personality and character. Although Chinese brushes are numbered, there is not always total consistency amongst the different makers. The centre brush in the illustration is a medium-sized one. The bristles are approximately 1 inch (2.5 cm) in length. The cost of brushes varies according to both the size and the type of hair used in the brush.

An assortment of brushes, from small to large, is also shown.

Some are hanging from a special rack (only to be used when the brushes are completely dry); a multiple brush, made up of ten small brushes glued together and used for washes, is lying on a wooden polished brush rest; a bamboo 'fountain brush' with its cap at its side is available for calligraphy; a set of six matching brushes demonstrates the range of brush sizes available and helps show the comparison between the popular sized brushes and the huge brush lying next to them.

The Chinese brush always returns to a fine point when it is wet, but its uniqueness lies in its versatility. If the painter wishes, the brush can produce strokes of varying degrees of broadness, or even split itself into two or more points to produce multiple lines with a single stroke. It is usual in ink painting only to use one brush throughout, as the brush will be capable of painting everything from the finest line to broad areas of wash. It is also extremely helpful in maintaining the unity of brushwork style in the painting to use only one brush.

13

The Chinese brush is made up of hairs of varying lengths, bound together in a very special way and set in a bamboo holder. It is built round a central core, increasing in circumference as layers of hair are added to the core. When the correct size has been reached, the bundle of hair is tied, glued and inserted into the open end of a bamboo handle. (Care has to be taken not to loosen the glue in these brushes, as this is its weakest point. Hot water should not be used for brush washing. If the hairs do come out of the handle, they usually remain tied together in the bundle and can be re-inserted and glued with a modern glue.) A brush from the Western world has a large amount of hair inside the handle, while the opposite is true for an oriental brush. This special construction enables the brush to behave in a unique way when loaded with ink.

The stages in making a brush

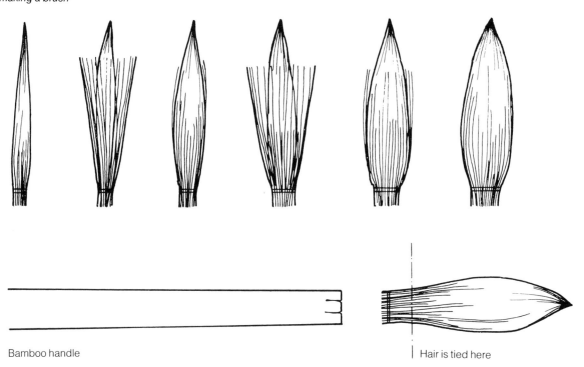

Bamboo handle

Hair is tied here

Preparing the Brush for Painting

Before actual painting can begin the Chinese brush has to be 'broken in' if it is a new one, not previously used.

First, the cap should be removed. This is sometimes bamboo, and nowadays may even be made of plastic. It should then be thrown away and not put back on the brush as its use was to protect the brush during its travels.

Next, the coating of starch, used to shape and protect the hairs, should be removed by dipping the brush in water and gently manipulating the point against the side of the paint dish, or even, very gently, massaging with the fingers.

Looking after the Brush

The brush should always be washed at the end of its use, taking special care to remove all traces of the black ink, which dries into a gritty state and would damage the brush if left in the hairs for a long time.

Brushes should be dried in the air by being laid down horizontally with the hairs suspended over the edge of a plate or ink stone. Traditionally, painters used a brush rest, often made in the shape of a mountain, to rest the damp brushes while in the process of painting. For Chinese painting it is important to be extra careful with excess water or dampness as the absorbency of the paper puts it more at risk than in ordinary Western watercolour painting. However, brushes should not be left to dry on the ink rest or the moisture seeps down to collect at the base of the hairs and may loosen the brush from the handle.

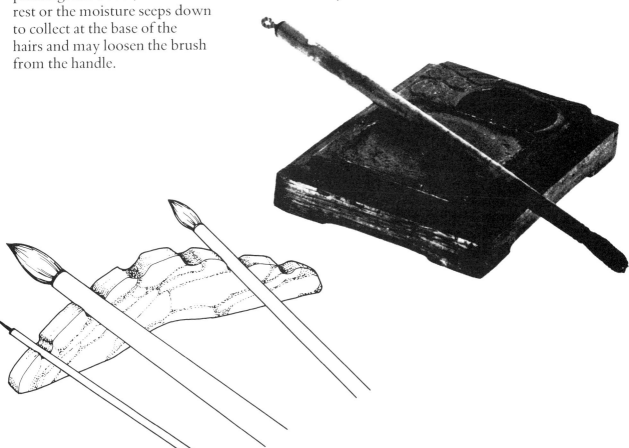

The Ink Stone

To make the black ink, the ink stick is rubbed in water on an ink stone. The grinding action rubs ink from the stick, enabling it to mix with the water. The finer the grain of the ink stone, the smoother the ink becomes and the longer the time needed for grinding.

The stone should be extremely smooth and hard. The most famous ink slabs are said to be from the Anhui district of China, where most are made from black stone, but there are also varieties with red or green markings forming designs in the stone.

Ink stones

The Ink Stick

Old Chinese ink is made of pine soot mixed with glue and other ingredients to hold it together. It comes compressed into the form of a stick, sometimes round, sometimes square, decorated with characters and pictures in gold. Other ink sticks are made from lampblack mixed with varnish, pork fat, and musk or camphor; these have a lightly bluish, metallic tinge to them. (Tradition says that if this ink stick is rubbed on the lips or tongue, it will act as a good remedy for fits and convulsions.)

A good ink stick is light in weight and very brittle. The best ink sticks produce a black which does not stick the brush hairs together, or fade with time.

The size of the ink stick should be compatible with the size of the ink stone on which it is to be rubbed and able to make an amount of ink suitable for the subject matter and painting size required.

Large bamboo paintings need a large ink stick, ink stone and brush; but a short piece of writing will not need so much ink to be made, so the stick and stone can be smaller.

The ink stick wears down very slowly with use, but the ink stone will last forever.

Mixing the Ink

Before beginning to paint, the artist always prepares fresh ink. Although Chinese ink is available in bottles, it is not suitable for painting; nor does it generate the variety of tones, from deepest black to delicate pearl grey, which can be produced by the Chinese ink stick. The action of rubbing the ink stick in the water on the ink stone has the psychologically meditative effect of

Different ink sticks

preparing the mind for the painting ahead, and as such has always been regarded almost as a sacred rite.

To mix the ink, first put some clear water into the well of the ink stone. Hold the ink stick upright and dip one end into the water to dampen it, then begin to rub it on the flat surface of the ink stone. (The amount of water depends upon how much ink you expect to need. Begin with about half a teaspoonful, then experience will help you to increase or decrease this.)

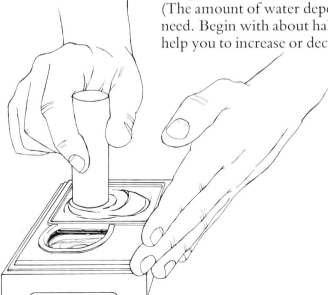

Rub the ink stick strongly on the stone in clockwise circles until the ink is thick and oily. When the rubbing motion seems to adhere, moisten the end of the stick again with water, or add an extra minuscule amount from a water dropper or tiny spoon. The ink is ready for use when it reaches an almost oily consistency, leaving trails behind on the stone's surface. By that time the rather abrasive noise of the grinding has become muffled and softer. As the water gradually evaporates, the mixture becomes slowly more concentrated.

Caring for the Ink Stick and Ink Stone

The ink stick should not be left to stand on the ink stone, or it will stick to it and damage the stone, therefore allow it to dry freely in the air. Old ink should not be left to dry and coagulate on the stone, as the gritty grains can spoil newly rubbed ink if they become mixed together. Gentle washing will keep the stone's surface clean.

The Painting Surface

With all the tools now assembled, the paper must be selected and then all the 'four treasures of the studio' will be ready and painting can begin. Chinese paper is available in many qualities and kinds. It was originally made from the bark of trees and old fishing nets, but is now made from rice-straw, reeds, wood pulp, etc. Some papers are sized and treated with glue, others are not. Altogether there are many types of paper with different levels of absorbency.

This absorbency is an essential quality of the paper. Individual papers – rice paper, mulberry or bamboo – react differently to the brush strokes, so the painting surface can have a determining effect on the style of the painting. The technique of the brush stroke is affected by whether the paper surface is rough, smooth, dull or glossy, more or less absorbent, so the techniques required may include a quicker brush stroke, a drier brush than usual, greater control of the ink, thicker brushwork and a more all-over style.

Sized paper allows for slower brushwork, as the ink does not run so quickly and it is also fast drying. Therefore, fine, detailed work is easier to accomplish on this type of paper.

Practice enables the painter to find out exactly how the brush and ink react with each different paper's absorbency. Since there is still a considerable amount of individual work required in the making of Chinese papers, the same type of paper may react differently with each different batch supplied. Even the weather, be it dry or humid, can affect the reaction or ink on the paper surface.

The painting paper, however, must be placed horizontally on a flat surface and held down by thin, flat weights. Underneath the Chinese paper, an absorbent layer, such as blotting paper or newspaper, is placed to take up any surplus ink.

Paper Thickness

Painting paper does vary considerably in thickness. The levels of absorbency are not directly proportional to the thickness of each of the differet kinds of paper, since the weave of the paper, whether it is open or closed, helps to affect the flow of ink through the paper. A piece of cleansing tissue is 3/1000 inch thick while one sheet of Chinese absorbent paper measures 2/1000 inch and others vary up to as much as 12/1000 inch, this being the thick *Hosho* paper.

The most versatile paper is available in a long continuous roll, approximately 25 yards (22 m) long. The most commonly used width is 17½ inches (44 cm) wide, although narrower rolls are also obtainable, some of them already divided into fixed lengths.

Usually Chinese paper has a 'smooth' and a 'rough' side which can easily be discovered by finger touch. The 'smooth' side is the correct one to use as the painting surface. The rolls of paper all have this smooth side as the *inside* surface of the roll, presumably as a way of giving it the maximum possible protection.

Various types of silk can also be used as a painting surface, but the best quality work in shades of black is always done on paper as the essence of ink painting is the reaction between the absorbency of the paper and the brush.

Holding the Brush

The adaptability of the Chinese brush is very much a result of the way in which it is held. The techniques are as dependent upon this as the sword stroke is to the manner of holding the sword. The brush is not held close to the bristles, but in the middle or at the top of the handle, depending upon the stroke being executed at the time. The hand should be unsupported and be able to move freely.

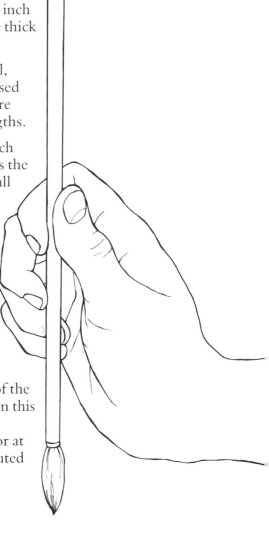

In ancient times the grip was not exactly the same as it is now. One book describes the moving of the ring and little fingers from the front to the underside of the brush as being as decisive a moment as the adoption of the stirrup in warfare. A totally different method was invented which gave a great deal more control to the movement of the brush and therefore produced a whole new range of painting.

The brush is held perpendicularly between thumb and index finger, with the middle finger also touching the brush behind and below the index finger. The ring finger supports the brush from the other side and the little finger supports the ring finger.

It is this combination of support from both sides that enables the artist to move the brush freely in all directions over the *flat* painting surface and still retain control over the movements of the brush.

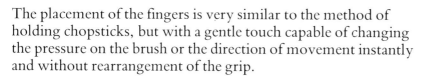

The placement of the fingers is very similar to the method of holding chopsticks, but with a gentle touch capable of changing the pressure on the brush or the direction of movement instantly and without rearrangement of the grip.

The brush can be held vertically or obliquely, but in all cases the grip remains the same. It is not an easy position to take, especially for those who have already had experience with Western brush techniques, but it is essential to correct handling of the brush in all its manifest and diverse facets.

The *upright brush position*, although it can only produce a line, can give a variable thickness according to the pressure which is put on it at the time of painting. If only the tip touches the paper lightly, the stroke will be a thin one; if pressure is applied, the stroke is broadened because of the extra bristles used. The tone will depend on the ink loading of the bristles further up the tip.

In the *oblique position*, the brush tip and the upper bristles move parallel to each other and their paths are separate so that quite a different effect is achieved.

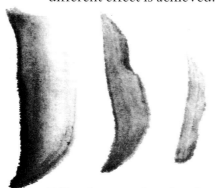

Effect is not only related to position and pressure, but also to the speed of the stroke. In the main, the broad stroke can be made at a slower pace than the thin stroke.

The essence of Chinese painting is contained within brush control. The skills involved come only with practice; with continuous involvement and increased concentration, an instinct develops which guides the brush into appropriate positions and enables the hand to apply correct pressures, thereby achieving the desired results.

Mixing Shades of Black

For more control over the shades it is necessary to mix the black ink deliberately into the shades rather than acquire them casually mixed together in the brush.

1 Using the brush, take some of the dark ink from the ink stone and put it on to the plate or porcelain dish. (The brush should be wet, but not dripping.)

2 Using the same brush, take water, a few drops at a time, from the water-holder to the plate and mix the water and ink together.

3 Test the resulting tone on a practice piece of paper. (Eventually this should not be necessary as experience will be the guide.)

4 If the tone is too dark, add some more water; if too light, then more ink is needed from the ink stone.

5 Black ink should always be used directly from the ink stone, but care must be taken that the brush is not too wet when this is done or it will automatically be diluted and reduced in tone.

6 When the shade, or shades, required have been made on the
   plate and the brush is to be loaded for the stroke, make sure
   once again that the brush is not already overloaded with water.

It is essential to be able to control the amount of water in the
brush. Over a period of time and practice, a 'feel' is acquired as to
the capacity of each individual brush to hold the ink, what the
tone is when looking at the colour of the brush, and when
re-loading is necessary because the brush has become too dry.
Eventually, seven differentiated shades of black can be made, but
for the beginner, five shades can be easily obtained from the
black ink stick. The diagram shows these shades, so that they can
be referred to in later chapters.

| 1 | 2 | 3 | 4 | 5 |

Loading the Brush

The capacity of the Chinese brush to hold water and ink is one of
its most important features. Strokes can only be executed
correctly and with control if the brush has been correctly loaded.
The amount of water in the brush controls the wetness of the
stroke. If the intention is to paint a brush stroke which flows
freely over the surface of the paper, but is still within the painter's
control, then it is not only important for the brush not to be too
wet (which can cause over-absorbency in the paper), but also for
it not to be too dry (which stops the brush flow and causes spaces
to appear in the brush stroke).

Shade 3

Lines
Shade 1

Shade 2

Shade 5

Shade 4

Shades represented on this lotus painting

Loading the brush with three tones. As an experiment in brush loading and a demonstration of the versatility of the Chinese brush, the following is a helpful exercise. First, make some black ink. Then:

1 Dip the brush in fresh, clean water.

2 Hold the brush upright to allow the surplus water to drip off.

3 Touch the tip of the brush to the darkest ink on the ink stone.

4 Allow the ink to rise up the bristles.

5 Press the bristles gently against the side of a clean plate or porcelain dish.

6 Touch the tip once again to the dark ink on the stone.

There should now be three tones on the brush; the darkest at the tip and the lightest tone nearest to the handle of the brush.

Now, put the whole of the brush bristles gently down on the Chinese paper and paint a line perpendicular to the handle of the brush. This oblique should show all three tones on the paper.

If the heel of the brush (nearest the handle) is lifted off the paper, then only two tones will remain on view.

This exercise also helps to show that the angle of the handle controls both the width of the stroke and the tones. If the brush is held upright, for instance, then only one tone will result. The ink put on the tip can, of course, be varied, but the tip of the brush, which can only draw a line, can only give one shade. However, with all the bristles on the paper a much wider range of tonal changes can be achieved.

Even using only one tone, quite different effects are obtained by

(a)   using a wet brush, or

(b)   using a dry brush.

It is not necessary to restrict practice to strokes alone. In fact it is more helpful to attempt small, but complete paintings, so that the individual strokes can be seen to combine with others in the overall composition of the brushwork.

The following chapters will demonstrate just a few of the ways that Chinese black ink, together with a Chinese brush, can convey myriad colours in the changing pageant of nature's beauty.

Bamboo

The bamboo grows as high as a tree and belongs to the same family as grass. Its stems – hard, straight and hollow – are always pointing upwards. Its leaves are green at all seasons and beautiful under all conditions – struggling beneath the winter snow or swaying with the storm, under the moon or in the sun.

Although bamboo is distributed throughout the subtropical and mild temperate zones, the heaviest concentration and largest number of species are to be found in South-East Asia. There are about 1,000 species of bamboo, some growing up to heights of between 100 and 120 feet (30 and 37 m) and having stems up to 12 inches (30 cm) in diameter.

Bamboo has always played a key role in Chinese culture and art and has helped generally to shape the country's life style. Poets and painters are inspired by bamboo's beauty and strength. Su Shih said, 'I would rather eat no meat than live without bamboo. The lack of meat will make me thin, but the lack of bamboo will make me vulgar.' During the Southern and Northern Dynasties, a group of seven men of letters were known as the Seven Wise Men of the Bamboo Grove, so wisdom came to be associated with bamboo. As the bamboo grows upright, weathering all conditions, so it came to represent the perfect gentleman who always remains loyal. Wen Cheng-ming wrote:

A pure person is like a tall bamboo;
A thin bamboo is like a noble man.

If any one subject area could be said to epitomise Chinese painting and in particular shades of black, then it would certainly be bamboo. The structure of bamboo is allied in many ways to the strokes required in Chinese writing. When painting there can be no hesitation as brush meets paper, since the power that propels the brush to action comes entirely from within. Tranquillity combined with confident brush control is needed to achieve a successful bamboo painting.

Because of the popularity of the subject matter, a great deal has been written about bamboo painting. The following is a compact version of the principles involved in this specific area of Chinese brush painting, where composition, brush control and ink tones are all essential elements of a successful bamboo painting.

Principles of Bamboo Painting – Composition

Bamboo is made up of *four* parts: the stem, the knot or joint, the branches and the leaves.

The Stems

1 Space should be left between the stem sections for the knots.

2 The sections between knots near the ends of the stems should be short, those forming the middle should be long, while at the base of the stem they are again short.

3 Avoid painting bamboo stems that appear withered, swollen, or too dark in tone.

4 The stems should not all be of the same height.

5 The edges of the stem should be distinct.

6 The knots should firmly join the sections above and below them, their forms being like half a circle.

7 At about the fifth knot above the soil, the branches and foliage begin to grow.

8 If only one or two stems of bamboo are being painted, the ink tones can all be the same.

9 If there are three or more stems, those in the foreground should be painted in dark tones and those in the back in light tones.

10 Avoid: (a) swollen or distorted stems; (b) uneven ink tones; (c) a dryness that looks like decay; (d) coarseness of texture; (e) a density of ink that may look like rot; and (f) equal spacing between knots.

Knots

1 The upper part of the knot should cover the lower, the lower part should support the upper.

2 Knots should not be too large or too small.

3 Knots should not be of equal size.

4 They should not be too curved.

5 The space between them should not be too large.

Branches

1 There are thick branches and thin branches growing from the main stems.

2 Thick branches have thin branches growing from the knots and are really a smaller version of the main bamboo stem.

3 Branches grow alternately from the knots of the stems and cannot grow from any other part of the bamboo plant.

4 In landscape painting, the bamboo is so thin that the branches look like stalks of grass.

Leaves

1 In painting leaves the brush should be saturated with ink.

2 The brush strokes should move easily and without hesitation.

3 The stroke requires a movement which is in turn light and then heavy.

4 If there are many leaves they should not be tangled.

5 If there are only a few leaves, then the branches should fill the blank spaces.

6 When bamboos are painted in the wind, their stems are stretched taut and the leaves give an impression of disorder.

7 Bamboos bend in the rain, but remain straight in fair weather.

8 In fair weather bamboo leaves compose themselves near a strong forked branch, with small leaves at the tip of the branches and groups of larger leaves near the base or body of the plant.

Five Essentials for Good Bamboo Painting

1 The silk or paper should be of good quality.

2 The ink should be fresh.

3 The brush should be swift and sure.

4 Before starting the composition should be clear in the mind, with each leaf and each branch mentally fixed in position.

5 All four sides of the bamboo should be considered when planning the composition.

Errors to Avoid

1 Avoid making stems like drumsticks.

2 Avoid making joints of equal length.

3 Avoid lining up the bamboos like a fence.

4 Avoid placing the leaves all to one side.

5 Avoid making the leaves like the fingers of an outstretched hand or the criss-crossing of a net, or like the leaves of a willow.

How to Paint Bamboo – Technique

The Stems

1 Make a *push stroke* from the bottom upwards.

2 The amount of bristle on the paper indicates the stem width, up to a maximum of the total length of the bristle.

3 With *light brush pressure*, place the brush on the paper and *pause, push, pause, off.*

4 The brush handle should be vertical.

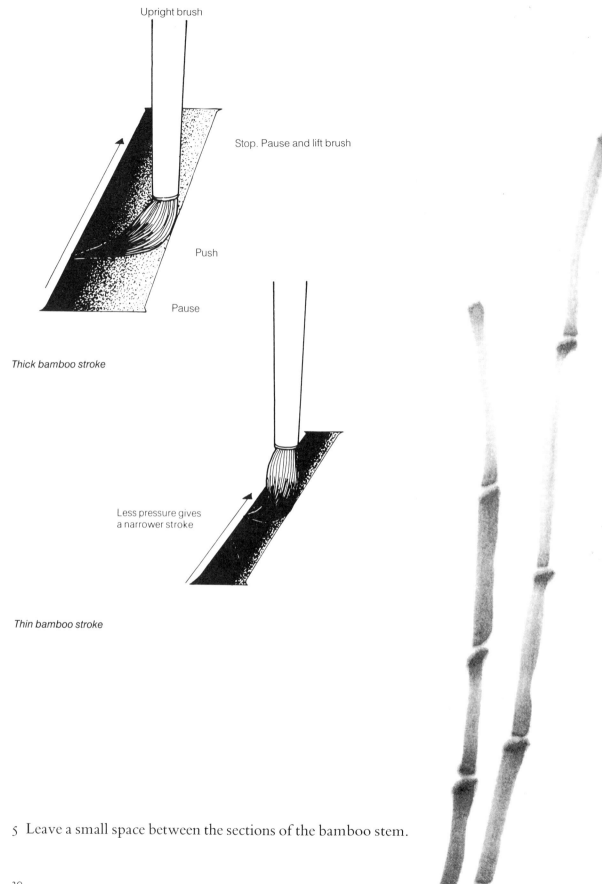

Upright brush

Stop. Pause and lift brush

Push

Pause

Thick bamboo stroke

Less pressure gives
a narrower stroke

Thin bamboo stroke

5 Leave a small space between the sections of the bamboo stem.

6 Double brush loading can be used to put a shadow
   directly on to the stem, as it is not possible to overpaint.

The knots or joints which divide the stem should be added in ink which is one shade darker than the stem itself. They should be added before the stem is dry. There are two methods of adding *joint strokes*:

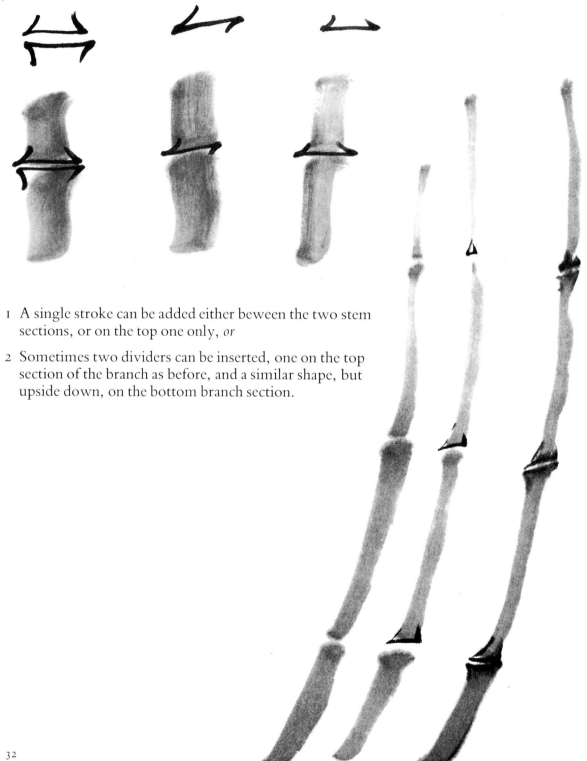

1 A single stroke can be added either beween the two stem sections, or on the top one only, *or*

2 Sometimes two dividers can be inserted, one on the top section of the branch as before, and a similar shape, but upside down, on the bottom branch section.

The Branches

There are different thicknesses of branches as there are of stems.

1 *Thin branches* grow from the main stems. The strokes, all painted upwards, should still have pauses, but because the branches are young, thin and leaf–bearing, they do not have joints.

2 *Thick branches* have thin branches growing from the knots and are really another smaller version of the main bamboo stems.

3 Branches grow alternately from the knots of the stems.

33

The Leaves

The leaves are always the last part of the bamboo plant to be
painted and are the most difficult part of the composition.
The groupings of the leaves can so easily appear clumsy, or
overcrowded, that it is advisable to practise leaf combinations on
their own before attempting to add them to the stems and
branches of the final bamboo composition.

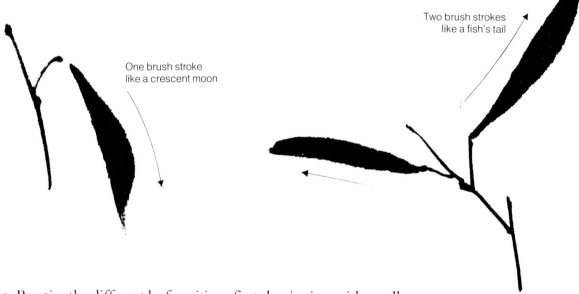

One brush stroke
like a crescent moon

Two brush strokes
like a fish's tail

1 Practise the different leaf positions first, beginning with small
   numbers of leaves.

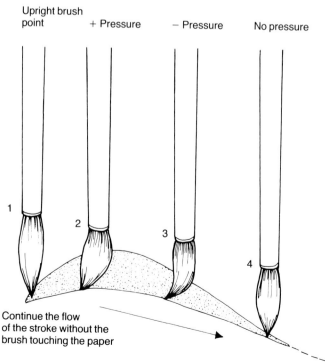

Upright brush
point

+ Pressure

− Pressure

No pressure

1

2

3

4

Continue the flow
of the stroke without the
brush touching the paper

2 Leaves can be painted upwards, or hanging down, depending on the general disposition of the main bamboo composition. Usually small groups tend to have all the leaves painted in the same direction.

3 If the leaves overlap, then care must be taken not to overload the brush as two layers of ink are filling the same paper space. It is often easier to allow one group of leaves to dry before painting others on top of them.

Examples of spread-out leaves in groups of two and three

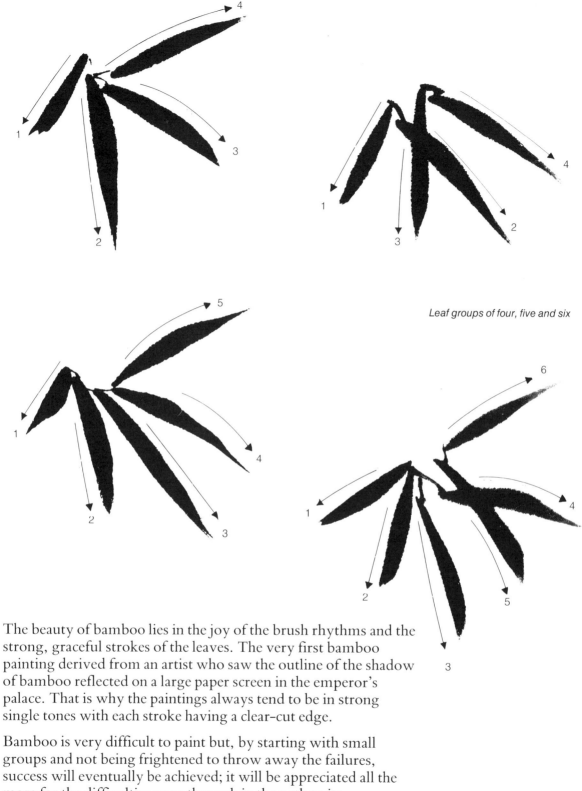

Leaf groups of four, five and six

The beauty of bamboo lies in the joy of the brush rhythms and the strong, graceful strokes of the leaves. The very first bamboo painting derived from an artist who saw the outline of the shadow of bamboo reflected on a large paper screen in the emperor's palace. That is why the paintings always tend to be in strong single tones with each stroke having a clear-cut edge.

Bamboo is very difficult to paint but, by starting with small groups and not being frightened to throw away the failures, success will eventually be achieved; it will be appreciated all the more for the difficulties gone through in the path to its attainment.

36

Calligraphy

The term calligraphy derives from the Greek work 'kalligraphia' which means beautiful writing. For the Chinese, the same high standards of brushwork apply to this art as apply to painting, for calligraphy is an art form itself.

Bone Carving Shang Dynasty (1766-1122 BC)	Large Seal Chou Dynasty (1122–256 BC)	Small Seal Ch'in Dynasty (221-207 AD)	Clerical Style Han Dynasty (207 BC-AD 220)	Standard Sui Dynasty (AD 588-present)

Three hills or rocks

Shan   Mountain

The branches, trunk and roots

Mu   Tree

First, head and arms, later, legs only

Jen   Man

Stream with eddies on either side

Shai   Water

A picture of the sun

Jih   Sun, day

Bone Carving Shang Dynasty (1766-1122 BC)	Large Seal Chou Dynasty (1122-256 BC)	Small Seal Ch'in Dynasty (221-207 BC)	Clerical Style Han Dynasty (207 BC-AD 220)	Standard Sui Dynasty (AD 588-present)

Head, scales and tail

Yu   Fish

Fingers and lines of the hand

Shon   Hand

An ancient vase containing wine

Yu   New wine

The connection between the art of writing Chinese characters and the art of painting is easier to understand when you consider that these characters were, at one time, actually pictures. The earliest mode of written communication was in the form of pictographs rather like the Egyptian hieroglyphics. When a more compex system of combining pictures evolved, it became ever more necessary to condense the pictorial forms into symbols or characters, where each one stood for a particular word.

The historical evolution of the written language explains the variety of styles found during the different dynasties. The earliest pictographs were found carved on bones and shells and were from the Shang Dynasty (1766-1122 BC). A more formalised large seal script developed during the Chou Dynasty (1122-256 BC) and was inscribed in bronze and stone. During the Ch'in Dynasty (221-207 BC) the small seal style, which is still used in seals today, was introduced by the calligrapher Li Ssu. Then followed the more formalised official style, sometimes called 'clerical', in use from the Han Dynasty (207 BC-AD 220) to the beginning of the Sui Dynasty (AD 588).

Within the period AD 588 to the present day, there have developed three types of writing which are used appropriately to their context:

Running   Standard   Grass   Symbols for 'moon' in three styles

To be able to write some Chinese characters on a painting – the date or a good luck symbol, or perhaps a small poem – is the easiest way to begin to attempt Chinese calligraphy. Later it may be possible to make the calligraphy the whole focus and main element of the composition but, of course, it is always very difficult to write with confidence in a foreign language.

The importance of calligraphy in Chinese life cannot be underestimated. Scrolls of calligraphy are traditionally offered as gifts and they are used as wall-hangings, hand scrolls and album leaves in the same manner as paintings. The two arts share a common origin and each evolved as a means of making an aesthetic statement, expressing the underlying principles of nature.

The Chinese characters, the written symbols of the Chinese language, are usually made up of several parts. Each part of the character is called 'a component'. (Some 'components' are characters in their own right.) Each component is composed of a number of basic strokes and the following are the seven most elementary ones.

The arrows show the direction of the brush movement:

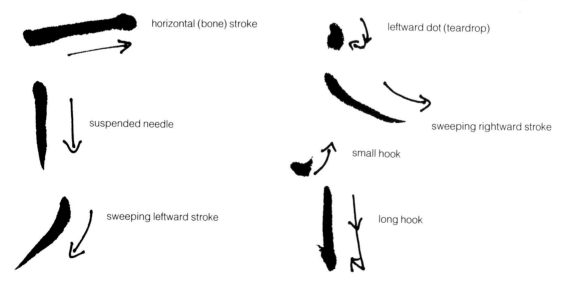

horizontal (bone) stroke

leftward dot (teardrop)

suspended needle

sweeping rightward stroke

small hook

sweeping leftward stroke

long hook

The Main Strokes Involved in Calligraphy

Hook Stroke

Angle the brush handle away from yourself at approximately 45°.
Point the brush tip to the top left-hand corner of the paper.
Put brush to paper, then drag from left to upper right, gradually
lifting off.

Teardrop Stroke

Hold the brush vertically, press quickly to lower right, pause and
rotate.

Bone Stroke

This stroke is the Hook and Teardrop combined, but lengthened
in between.

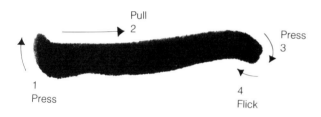

The basic structure of each character is balanced and logical and
each stroke follows the other in a precise and rhythmic order. The
general rule is to work from the top down, and from left to right
within each character. The successive characters are placed in
vertical rows, starting at the top of the paper and at the right-hand
side. Each new row begins at the top and is placed to the left of the
previous one.

Although everyday Chinese writing is now done horizontally, it
is still eminently acceptable for poems, couplets or decorative
writing on paintings to retain the old format of vertical lines.

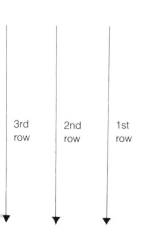

The individual strokes already described should be practised first,
with the painter sitting in a very erect position, or standing, if the
work is to be particularly large. The brush should be kept upright
and, to allow for totally free movement of the arm, the wrist
should not be allowed to rest on the surface of the paper.

The ink used should be a rich, strong black; the brush loaded
thoroughly but without being super-saturated.

Remember to increase the pressure to broaden the stroke and release it to obtain a narrower line. Try to develop graceful hooking strokes, carefree but strongly formed sweeping strokes and well-proportioned but self-contained long strokes. Boldness is required for the dots and short strokes.

As with all the Chinese brushwork, confidence has to be developed by practice. A bold, sure touch is a necessity for successful calligraphy. No possibility of erasing, altering or obliterating is available for the Chinese calligrapher, but constant practice using the brush will eventually develop the expertise required. Unlike other areas of Chinese painting, where individual stroke practice is not encouraged, calligraphy does need special attention to be paid to the basic strokes of the character component.

Developing from this, the quality of the brushwork is judged, not only by the length and thickness of the individual strokes, but also by how the strokes meet each other as they are written in sequence to form each character.

Rules of stroke order in writing Chinese characters are as follows:

Example	Stroke order	Rules
十	一 十	horizontal before vertical
大	尢 大	left before right
外	夕 外	from top to bottom
你	亻 你	left component before right component
月	冂 月	from outside to inside
国	冂 囲 国	inside precedes the sealing (closing) stroke
小	亅 小 小	middle precedes the two sides

Most of these rules and the basic stroke elements are contained within the much used character for 'long life'. This character, *shou* (pronounced show), is to be found as a single decorative piece of calligraphy on a scroll, as an embroidery motif, on pottery and contained within many written expressions of general goodwill on Chinese New Year cards. It can most usefully be tried as the first calligraphic painting motif, after the individual strokes have been practised.

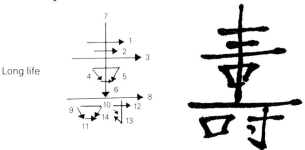

Long life

Follow the arrow directions and paint the strokes in the order as shown. It often helps to vary the size of the character to find which particular format suits you best for practice purposes.

Another popular character is 'luck' which is *Fu* (pronounced *foo*). Again, the arrows give both direction and order of stroke, so that the character will develop rhythmically as it is painted.

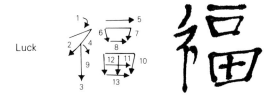

Luck

If one stroke does not quite join on to the next, it is much better to leave the slight gap than to attempt to add an extra piece to the character, and of course, as always with traditional Chinese painting, strokes cannot be successfully 'tidied up' if the brush technique has caused an incorrect stroke to be formed. No amount of description can substitute for the marvellous feeling of accomplishment when, after many faulty practice pieces, one character, or even one stroke, appears faultlessly on the absorbent painting surface.

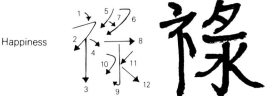

Happiness

The addition of the character for 'happiness' to the two already described will enable the painter to write 'All Good Wishes – luck, happiness and long life'.

All good wishes

Another small but useful series of characters is the set of Chinese numbers, plus the characters for month and year necessary to enable the date to be written. A painting seems to be more finished if it is dated and the small number of characters necessary to achieve this are as follows.

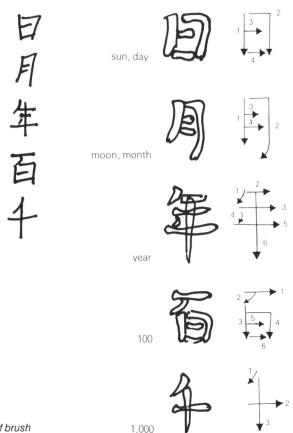

sun, day

moon, month

year

100

1,000

Line and arrow diagrams indicate order of painting and direction of brush

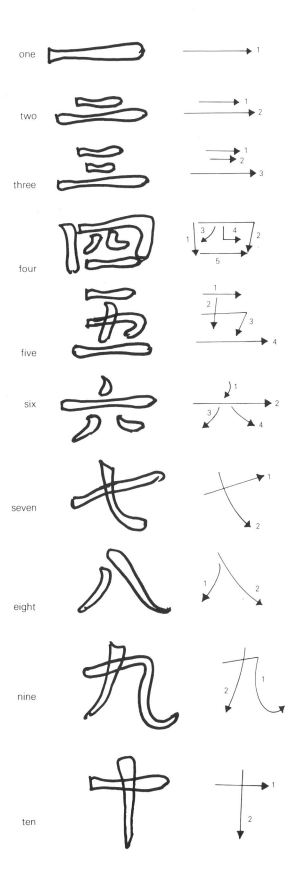

one

two

three

four

five

six

seven

eight

nine

ten

one	
thousand	
nine	
hundred	
nine	
ten (eighty)	
four	
year	1994

To begin with this may be sufficient, but if more accuracy and precision are required then the month and the day can be added.

comma	
five (fifth)	
month	
comma	
six (sixth)	
day	

Written characters in their pictorial form were the forerunners of today's calligraphy and also of traditional painting. They appeared on bronze vessels and probably at about the same time as embroidery motifs, with particular attention being paid to the character of the silk cocoon. Chinese embroidery pieces have examples of Chinese script worked on them, from single characters to full-length poems, producing designs rich in symbolism as well as pleasing aesthetically and intellectually.

Since most ancient embroidery was made as an adornment for the robes of male officials, the longevity character – *shou* – appeared frequently, but the most popular character on old embroidered pieces was 'the double *hsi*' – double happiness:

One 'good wish phrase' also popular on embroidery seems to sum up the far-ranging influence of calligraphy as an art form, embodying, as it does, a wealth of ancient philosophy in a minimum of writing. The seal character inscription shown reads 'Wu fu chin ju': 'May you have the five blessings and embody the nine similarities (in your person)'. The 'five blessings' are long life, wealth, health, many sons and a natural death. On the right is the modern form.

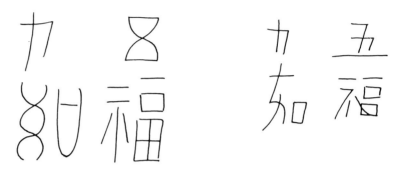

The 'nine similarities' are embodied in the following wish: 'Like high hills, like mountain masses, like top-most ridges, like huge bulks of rock, like streams, like the morn, like the sun, like the age of the southern hills and like the luxuriance of fir and cypress, so may be thy increase and descendants to come.'

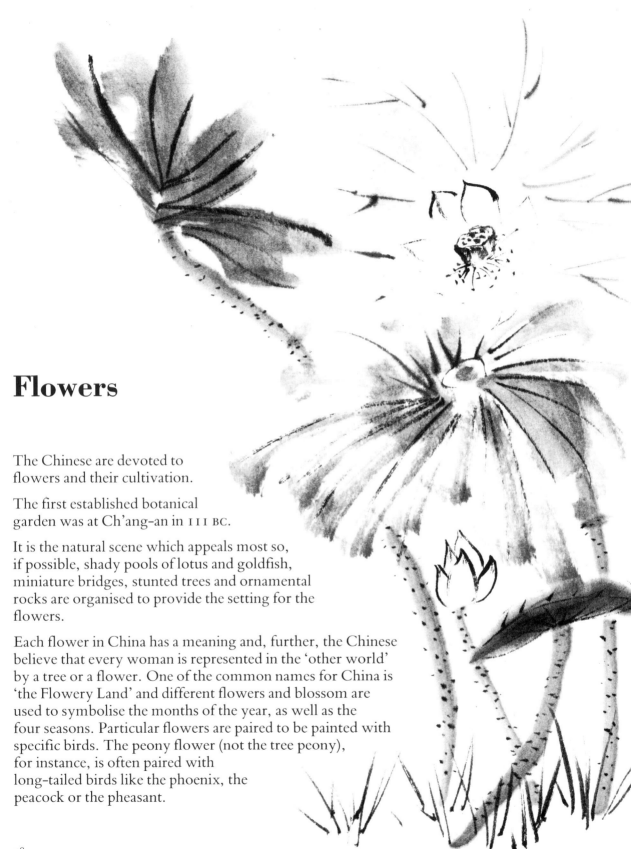

Flowers

The Chinese are devoted to flowers and their cultivation.

The first established botanical garden was at Ch'ang-an in I I I BC.

It is the natural scene which appeals most so, if possible, shady pools of lotus and goldfish, miniature bridges, stunted trees and ornamental rocks are organised to provide the setting for the flowers.

Each flower in China has a meaning and, further, the Chinese believe that every woman is represented in the 'other world' by a tree or a flower. One of the common names for China is 'the Flowery Land' and different flowers and blossom are used to symbolise the months of the year, as well as the four seasons. Particular flowers are paired to be painted with specific birds. The peony flower (not the tree peony), for instance, is often paired with long-tailed birds like the phoenix, the peacock or the pheasant.

The chart shows the symbolism and groupings of the different
flowers and blossoms throughout the year.

Chinese floral calendar and flower symbolism

Flowers for the 12 seasons	Seasons	Seasonal flowers	Flowers symbolising	Accompanying animals/designs	Secondary characteristics
1 Prunus	Spring symbol:	Almond	Womanly beauty	Court ladies	Fortitude in sorrow
	the Tree	Bellflower	Happiness, good luck	God of wealth	Success/fame
2 Peach	Peony	Cherry	Womanly beauty, youth	Young people	Virility, hope
		Millet	Plenty, strength	Quails, partridge	Perennial effort
		Narcissus	Good fortune	Fairy beings	Introspection, self-esteem
3 Peony		Peach	Spring, youth, marriage, immortality	Bride & attendants	Good wishes, riches
4 Cherry		Willow	Meekness, feminine grace, charm	Swallow	Poetic ability, artistic worth
5 Magnolia	Summer symbol:	Aster	Beauty, charm	Butterflies	Humility
	the	Azalea	Womanly grace	Butterflies	Luxuriant abilities
	Lotus	Camellia	Beauty, good health	Dragonflies	Physical & mental strength
6 Pomegranate		Convolvulus	Love & marriage	Humming birds	Early day, dependence
7 Lotus		Iris	Grace, affection	Bees	Beauty in solitude
		Jasmine	Grace, sweetness	Butterflies	Fragrance, attraction
		Lotus	Summer, purity, fruitfulness	Duck	Spiritual grace
8 Pear		Magnolia	Feminine beauty	Bees	Ostentation, self-esteem
		Peony	Love, beauty, spring, youth	Phoenix, peacock, pheasant	Royalty, pre-eminence
9 Mallow		Pomegranate	Posterity, offspring	Playing children	Natural abundance
		Rose	Fragrance, prosperity	Bees, humming birds	Sweetness in desolation
10 Chrysanthemum	Autumn symbol:	Chrysanthemum	Mid-autumn, joviality, ease	Crab, dragon, girls	Scholarship, retirement
	the	Gardenia	Feminine grace, subtlety	Swifts	Artistic merit
	Chrysanthemum	Mallow	Quietude, rusticity	Martins, geese	Peace, humility
		Myrtle	Fame, success	God of wealth, officials	Humility in achievement
		Oleander	Beauty, grace	Birds, insects	Joy, achievement
		Olive	Grace, delicacy	Wild geese	Quiet persistence, strength
11 Gardenia		Pear	Purity, justice	Officials in robes	Unswerving judgement
12 Poppy	Winter symbols:	Almond	Womanly beauty	Court ladies	Fortitude in sorrow
	Prunus	Fungi	Long life, immortality	Old man, young boys	Persistence
	and	Pine	Long life, courage	Stork	Immortality, faithfulness
	Poppy	Plum	Winter, long life, strength	Stork, white crane	Hardiness, triumph
		Poppy	Striking beauty, rest	White bear	Retirement, success

49

Painting Flowers

There is an accepted order for painting flowers the Chinese way. The flower heads themselves are painted first, then the leaves and lastly the stems. These rules have special exceptions in that grass orchids have their leaves painted first and blossom is not regarded as 'a flower' in the same way as, say, a lily or lotus. Most Chinese traditional artists begin by painting the most important element of the subject matter. It is, therefore, realistic to consider that for a plant this would be the flower itself; for blossom, it is the branch which is most dominant; and the elegance of a grass orchid is provided by the special overlapping of its long, thin leaves.

As there are basically two methods of painting – the outline method and the solid-stroke technique – a choice has to be made as to which of the two to use for different flower compositions. Most flowers can be painted in either technique or a combination of the two methods. That is to say, there are three ways:

1 All outline.
2 Outline flowers and solid-stroke leaves.
3 All solid strokes.

Each of these alternatives produces a different emphasis in the completed painting. Flowers which are painted totally in outline may be described as 'light' in emphasis, as it is the brush point only which touches the paper. At the other extreme, when the flowers, leaves and stems are all painted in the solid-stroke technique, the composition has a stronger feeling to it, since much more of the brush head has been applied to the painting surface. Tradition has built up a series of accepted combinations for specific flowers, although there are certainly no rules governing the choices made.

Most outline technique flowers are painted in black, but the solid-stroke techniques are often more suitable to colour painting, except in the case of a very important and positive flower such as the lotus.

Narcissus

To demonstrate the *outline technique*, a most suitable flower is the narcissus. The Shu-hsien, Water Immortal or narcissus is first mentioned in the ninth century as coming from Fu-lin, Byzantium. In late winter, when the Chinese celebrate the Spring Festival, they prepare feasts and decorate their houses with flowers and plants, their favourite for this purpose being the narcissus.

The delicate, narrow, emerald-green leaves, large white flowers, golden coronas and silvery-white roots provide an elegant background to the festivities and their delicate fragrance adds to the atmosphere.

The narcissus once grew wild along the marshes of the south-east coast of China becoming a cultivated flower in the tenth century. There are many varieties of narcissus, which divide into the single flowered category which has six petals, or the bunch-flowered variety which has a corona of split petals clustered in a ball-shape.

The Chinese believe that the colour, the fragrance and the elegance of this flower liken it to an ancient poem or painting.

Before beginning the painting, it is always important to organise the composition in the mind as fully as possible, while carefully rubbing the ink stick on the ink stone.

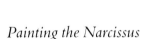

Painting the Narcissus

1 Load the tip of the brush only with black ink directly from the ink stone.

2 Beginning with the most central flower, paint its centre and then each petal starting from the inside of the flower.

3 Next, mix the black ink with some water on the palette and with dark grey paint the outline of the thicker section of the stem nearest to the flower.

4 Next the bulb is painted with its roots.

5 Finally, the long elegant leaves are painted in dark ink.

The composition, which clearly shows white flowers in their elegant simplicity, can be left as complete at this stage, or have shades of grey (or colour) added. The shades should not be added too carefully, as the intention is not merely to 'fill in the outline' but to add more depth to the painting; and care should be taken that all the outlines are dry before adding these shades.

To demonstrate the alternative, the outline flower and solid-stroke leaf method of painting flowers, the best example is the Chinese lotus.

Lotus

To the Chinese, the lotus is the most important of all the cultivated flowers, grown for both its beauty and its usefulness. It has large blossoms, tinted pink, creamy white or yellow, growing on stalks 6 or 7 feet (2 or 2.3 m) high, appearing from the centre of very broad (sometimes 3 feet (1 m) in diameter), nasturtium-shaped leaves.

Every part of this plant has a special use: the fruits and leaves are used as food; the dried yellow stamens are used as an astringent and as a cosmetic; the seeds can be used as medicine or eaten as a dessert. The kernels are boiled in soup, roasted or eaten raw, while the stems are sliced and boiled. The leaves can be taken medicinally or used dried to wrap food.

The lotus is also known as a symbol of purity and perfection, growing out of the mud into a state of blossoming beauty and fruitfulness. The flowers are open for a mere three days, then petal by petal they disintegrate, leaving the green seed head exposed.

It has become very positively connected to Buddhism, partly because of the symbolism; partly because of the visual representation of the Wheel of the Law by the flower form, with the petals taking the place of the spokes. Buddha is usually represented as seated on the sacred lotus and, in imitation of this,

Buddhist priests have developed the 'lotus posture' – a cramped position which develops a state of bodily peace. The flower is also one of the 'eight treasures', said to be auspicious signs seen on the sole of Buddha's foot.

It is not only as a symbol important to Buddhists that the lotus is recognised, but also as an emblem of one of the Eight Immortals of Taoism – the other main Chinese religion. The seed–cup on the lotus stem, with its many seeds, becomes an emblem of offspring.

The lotus is also regarded as representing summer and fruitfulness; it appears in stylised form in paintings, in embroidery, on carpets and as ceramic decorations.

Although it is not an easy flower to paint, mainly because of the disproportionate size of the leaves and the fact that the Western painter may well never have seen a lotus bloom, it is the most important flower in Chinese traditional painting and as such is well demonstrated by the power and versatility of shades of black.

Painting the Lotus

1 Plan the composition so that spaces are left for crossing leaves and stems.

2 Paint the pod heads first by outlining the seed pod and the tiny circular seeds.

3 Seed pods on their own should have a space left at the base so that the stalks can be joined correctly.

4 If the seed pods are still surrounded by the petals of the flower, then the petals grow from the base of the pod and overlapping must be planned before the outlines are painted.

5 The flower petals are finely veined and, although it is not necessary to show them, light-toned, thin ink lines can be included.

6 The leaves can be shown in various stages and positions
   as they unfold.

7 On the large leaves, the veins radiate from the
   centre of each leaf and alternate veins 'fork' as they
   approach the leaf edge.

8 The leaf stalks are darker than the flower stalks.

Stem

Leaf

Veins added

Dots added to stem

Grass

9 Each flower, bud and leaf has its own individual stalk.

Lotus bud almost open

Fully open flower

Peony

The tree peony is regarded as the king of flowers, the flower of riches and honour, and has been held in high esteem by the Chinese since the T'ang Dynasty.

It is an emblem of love and affection, a symbol of feminine beauty, and also represents the season of spring. The peony is sometimes called the 'flower of wealth and rank'. From the Sung period onwards it has often been a favourite pottery motif, both on its own and in composition with rocks.

If the plant becomes loaded with flower heads and heavily leafed in green this is regarded as an omen of good fortune; but if the leaves dry up and the flowers suddenly fade, this presages poverty for the flower's owner, or even some appalling disaster to the whole family.

Flowering plants are divided into two kinds: those with woody stems, usually perennials, and herbaceous plants which are usually annuals.

Painting the Peony

Following the painting of the narcissus as an all-outline flower, and the lotus, which was painted in the combined techniques of outline flower and solid-stroke leaves, the third technique is to

paint the flowers and leaves all in the solid–stroke method.
The peony is a good example of this method as it lends itself to the
impressionistic looseness of the brush strokes, in contrast to
the carefully constructed neatness of outline flowers.

The flower itself is large and heavy, not delicate, and is well
shown by the techniques of shades of black.

*Peony flower heads are very heavy. Notice how closely
the flowers grow to the leaves.*

The order of painting for the peony is: flower first, followed by leaves, and finally the stems are added. It is usual to begin at the centre of the flower, whether the flower is fully open or half open. Petals can be painted in a light shade of grey first, with strokes being superimposed in darker shades while the first brush strokes are still wet. The peony has petals darker at the outside and lighter in the middle, with each petal having a very ragged edge.

The peony plant has its leaves grouped in threes at the end of a stem which is connected to the main one.

Centre brush point

Brush point should always be to the centre

Add another petal layer in a lighter tone

Add more petals to the top or bottom of the flower head, depending in which direction you wish the head to point.

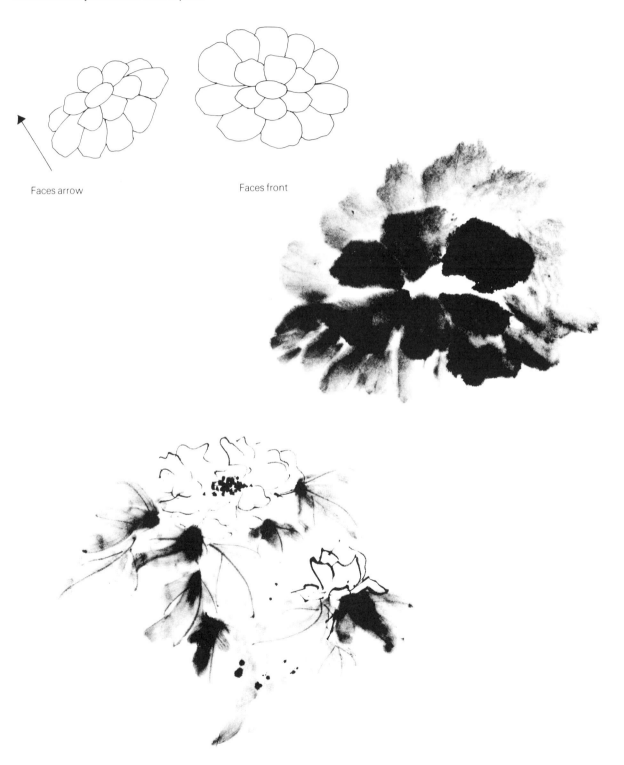

Faces arrow

Faces front

1

2

3

Add veins in black with tip of brush

For peony leaves use a medium wet brush and paint in groups of three.

Group 1

A peony leaf group

Group 3

Group 2

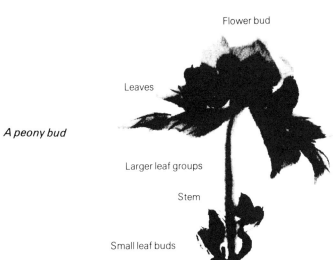

Flower bud

Leaves

A peony bud

Larger leaf groups

Stem

Small leaf buds

Insects

Bees, wasps, butterflies and other insects can be added to flower and blossom paintings to add life and a touch of realism to the composition. Insects gather round the flowers, collecting their fragrance; they climb along stems and alight on leaves. They can be used to hint subtly at the advent of spring, summer or autumn, by their very presence. Butterflies in spring have pliant wings and enlarged lower parts of a body about to lay eggs. In autumn, butterflies have strong wings, lean bodies and tails lengthened with age. Flying butterflies have their tube-like mouth appendage curled, but, alighted on a plant, the mouth extends to penetrate the flower and draw its nectar. Although insects, including butterflies, are usually placed in flower paintings as an ornamental addition, nevertheless due regard should be paid to the season, to maintain a certain degree of realism.

Painting Insects

There are two methods of painting insects, either with the outline or solid-stroke method. Solid strokes contain both wet and dry techniques (*dry* for the soft wings and head); *wet* for the top of the head, the eyes and the hard shiny legs). Bees are often added, if ink has been splashed, to cover up the mistake. As the Chinese bee is smaller than foreign varieties and is regarded by the Chinese as being an emblem of industry and thrift, it makes a very suitable addition to flower paintings.

Order for Painting Insects (except some butterflies)

1 Head

2 Body and wings

3 Legs and antennae

Bees and wasps

1 Insects usually have four wings and six legs.

2 Jumping insects have strong back legs and flying insects have large main wings.

3 When flying, an insect's body drops, but its wings point up.

4 An insect's legs are pulled up while flying.

5 When alighting an insect stretches its legs.

Notes on Painting Insects

1 A small pointed brush should be used.

2 Hair-line strokes are needed, with even more delicate brushwork for really small insects.

3 The order of painting is eyes, head, thorax, abdomen, wings, legs and antennae.

4 The head of the insect (to be painted first) needs a dark shade of ink, with the eyes always black.

5 Paint the wings of a flying insect with a dry brush, working from the base of the wing where it joins the body and allowing it to fade outward.

6 Fuzzy insects such as a bumble bee need a dry brush.

7 Shiny insects like wasps or beetles need a wet brush.

8 Solid insects have their legs painted in a series of fine bone-type (like calligraphy) strokes with a wet brush and black ink.

9 Each antenna should be painted in one smooth stroke.

Dragonflies

The dragonfly is an emblem of summer and a symbol of instability and weakness. It is often used in flower pictures, particularly those associated with water like the lotus.

As these insects appear in large numbers before a storm, they are sometimes known as the 'typhoon fly', while the Chinese slang term for them is 'old glassy' because of their large transparent wings. They flit over streams and along river banks, eating harmful insects, and are, therefore, much appreciated by the people who live near water.

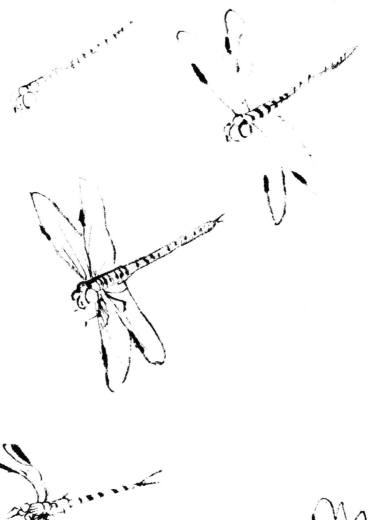

Dragonflies

Butterflies

The butterfly is not only a symbol of summer; it is also regarded as an emblem of joy, since the Chinese philosopher Chuang Tsu once had a dream in which he became a butterfly, happily flying from flower to flower sipping nectar. The same Taoist philosopher regarded the butterfly as a sign of conjugal felicity, perhaps the Chinese version of Cupid.

Although when painting insects, the head is usually painted first, this is not always so in the case of solid–stroke butterflies. Since the wings are the most important part of the insect they are painted first.

Order for painting butterflies

Special Notes on Butterflies

1 When flying, only half the body is visible.

2 At rest, the whole body is visible.

3 The butterfly has two antennae on its head.

4 The mouth is in between the antennae.

5 Flying in the morning, a butterfly's wings are straight up opposite each other.

Before a Chinese artist begins to paint, many hours have been spent in watching butterflies, for instance, or looking at the different varieties of insects, in flight and at rest. Every single element of nature is worthy of time and attention to the artist who wishes to portray, albeit impressionistically, the real, living world. The descriptions given here and the painting instructions for insects may seem to be very formal, but they should only be regarded as an aid, not a substitute, for the artist's own eyes. One of the accrued benefits of an interest in Chinese traditional painting is that a better and more intense way of looking at things develops unobtrusively. Seeing, instead of merely looking, becomes an everday occurrence. Even in the centre of a big city, there are bees and other insects to be seen and admired. The painting should follow the observation, so the ideas and information put forward in this section are only a pointer as to where and how to look, if this is the area of interest which fascinates you most.

Birds

Birds are rarely painted by themselves. They sit on the branch of a
tree, pause near a flower or rest at the side of a watery pool. They
help give life and movement, albeit gentle, to the calm, unruffled
serenity of the traditional Chinese flower and blossom paintings.
They also refer symbolically to character traits or imply unstated
associations. A crane suggests longevity (the Chinese believe
that the bird lives to 1,000 years of age), so for an old man's
birthday, a crane under a pine tree is considered lucky.

Mandarin ducks and swallows often occur in pairs – ducks on a water lily pond or swallows among willow trees mean happy matrimony. Ten magpies are a very lucky omen and usually appear in large official celebratory paintings.

Painting Birds

The Chinese say 'To paint a bird, do not go away from the form of an egg'. A bird begins life in the egg and that is also the basic body shape. Two egg-shaped ovals provide the framework for the bird.

Birds are hatched from eggs and their shape closely follows that of an egg, with head, tail, wings and feet added. The tail grows at the end of the oval.

If the bird is divided into three sections, the third section is where the legs go.

If a bird is divided into five sections, the wings are in the upper three sections.

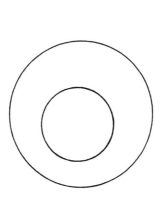

The small circle, which represents the head, can be moved inside or outside the body egg shape.

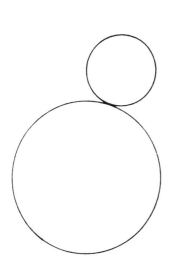

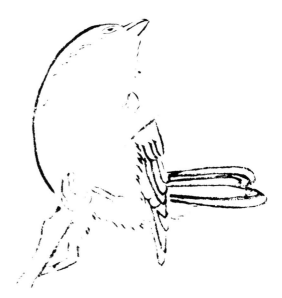

The preceding pictures give the general body shape and format. However, when starting to paint the bird there is an accepted Chinese order of painting which has to be followed. Since the bird must first be able to eat and then to see, the first part of the bird to paint is the bill. Next, paint the eye that is near the roof of the bill.

Although, occasionally, the eye can be painted before the beak, the eyes and beak are *always* painted before the body of the bird. Following the beak and the eyes, the head should be completed, then the bird's back, wing feathers, breast feathers, tail, legs and feet.

The two diagrams explain the order for both the 'brush-line' and 'solid-stroke' methods of painting birds. The bird can then be placed on a branch or in a tree as appropriate. Both methods use a fine brush for the beak, eyes and claws.

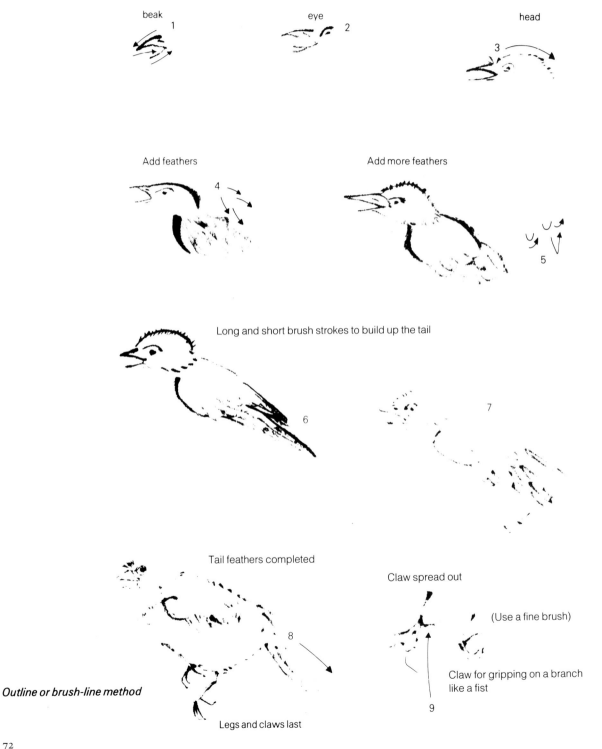

beak
1

eye
2

head
3

Add feathers
4

Add more feathers
5

Long and short brush strokes to build up the tail
6
7

Tail feathers completed
8

Claw spread out

(Use a fine brush)

Claw for gripping on a branch like a fist
9

Outline or brush-line method

Legs and claws last

Solid-stroke method. Fine brush *for eyes, beak and claws.* Medium brush *for head, body and feathers.*

Birds give life to a painting of a rather static branch, or tree, and can, therefore, be painted in a rather quiet, indistinct way. Alternatively, the bird can form the main element of the painting and, as such, will be required to demonstrate rather more of its own character. Some painters are expert in the art of depicting two or more birds in natural interaction in a fine and detailed manner, while Chai Pai Shih could convey the fluffiness of a baby chicken with three wet brush strokes.

As with all other subjects in traditional Chinese painting, it is necessary to observe and enjoy birds in their natural habitat until a clear picture can be retained in the mind, before attempting to commit brush to paper. This observation of nature is a pleasure in itself and one of the many side benefits to be obtained from the study of this ancient oriental art form.

The Chinese are so enamoured of their birds that, like a pet, they take them out for talks, either still in their cages, or perhaps sitting on their shoulder.

This bird has space below and may fly down into the picture

Composition

Arrange your flower and bird paintings so that they both look natural. In some places things may appear crowded, in other areas of the picture there may be much open space. According to the ancient Chinese, 'Where expansiveness is required, let there be room for a trotting horse, where compactness is required, let not a needle pass through'.

This bird has space to fly upwards

By putting the bird in one corner of the composition, he has the space to fly into the whole area

Roses

An Introduction to Chinese Colour Painting

Colour

The ideal paint for use in a Chinese painting is that made from natural minerals pounded up and combined with clear glue and boiling water. Nowadays, however, scientific progress has been such that we no longer need to resort to such a long and difficult process. Special Chinese colour sticks can be purchased with the four basic elemental colours (without black) and an additional blue stick. These are ground on a grey stone in the same way as the black ink stick. Sometimes a china plate or tile can be used to grind off the colour, which is softer in consistency than the black ink stick.

Colours: ink sticks, tubes and ceramic pots

These colours are pure and ideal for use on both paper and silk, but the tubes of Chinese water colours are also satisfactory. As far as modern Western proprietary brands of water colour are concerned, testing is advisable, because occasionally the man-made additives which help to produce colour fastness, or maintain the paint freshness, are themselves the cause of running in absorbent paper.

Use of Colour

Water colours must not be used thickly on absorbent paper – it is essential to mix the paint with water to the correct consistency for each individual stroke. Chinese white is often used to give depth to another colour and black can be a great help in providing a natural tint to leaves and stems or to darken colours.

It is also possible to load two or three colours at once on to a Chinese brush, so that the tones and shades are achieved in one stroke. This is explained on page 86.

Lotus

Poinsettia

A suitable flower with which to begin is the poinsettia. Since everyone 'sees' colours differently it is important for the initial emphasis to be on the brush strokes, not on the colour or the difficulties of balancing five equal petals in the correct proportion.

With the brush loaded with red water colour, fix the position of the centre of the first flower and, painting from the growing point, work generally in the order shown above. All petals, short or long, should be painted starting from the flower's centre. Re-load the brush when required. Petals must *not* overlap, otherwise too much liquid will overload the absorbent paper and the paint will spread in an uncontrolled manner. The water colour paint should be diluted so that when the brush is correctly loaded light and shade will be already contained in the stroke. The tip of the brush will normally contain darker colour than the other end of the bristles, particularly if the stroke is always commenced from an upright position.

Complete one flower before beginning the next one. The three-dimensional impression will be helped if you paint flower petals shorter on one side. Leaves can be painted in grey, or alternatively mix some colour such as green or blue with some light ink. This time the brush should be loaded to a much wetter consistency so that a softer stroke will result. Paint the leaves as shown on page 82, adding the veins to the leaves with black taken directly from the ink stone and loaded on to the point of the brush only.

Sometimes it may be necessary to stop after painting a few leaves and put in the veins before going on to the next leaves. The speed of drying will vary with the type of paper being used and the prevailing atmospheric conditions. Add the veins, remembering to vary the position of the main vein to prevent monotonous shapes resulting.

For the stem, load the brush with dark grey, grey-green, grey-brown or any other suitable colour combination. As the brush is pushed towards its destination, be ready to remove it if there is a leaf or flower impeding its path and re-start the stem again on the other side of the obstruction. Since the general tendency is to practise flowers and leaves diligently, but omit to put the same amount of practice time in on the stems, often the following faults can occur:

1 Not loading the brush with sufficient ink (running out in the middle of the stem or a too dry stroke).

2 Loading with too much ink (stem is too wet and ink runs uncontrollably).

3 Non-positive stroke (hand shakes and so does the stem).

4 Not aiming the stem correctly towards the flower. (Try practising in the air before allowing the brush to touch the paper.)

5 Attempting to 'touch up' or join a broken stem or a 'too thin' stroke. (Better to leave a blank space than to do this.)

6 Parallel stem lines. (No cure – remember next time to think before you paint.)

7 Awkward appearance. (Stems should be near to each other at the beginning of the stroke.)

As you will realise, a lot of practise is needed to become confident in the production of good stems.

To complete the picture several more strokes are needed. First, the leaves are connected to the stems with a small casual, curving line as shown at the top of the page.

Then, place small black dots (the ink taken directly from the ink stone and loaded on to the tip of the brush only) at random on the stems, to indicate where a leaf has dropped off, or some other natural flaw has occurred. These are called 'mi dots' and, apart from their value to the beginner as a remedy for some accidental mistake, will detract attention from some of the stark, clean lines of a stem too carefully executed.

The flowers should now be absolutely dry and you can add small oval lines indicating the centre of the poinsettia. Since black lines are 'hard' they will stand away from the larger petals helping to create an effect of depth. Special care must be taken with these last strokes as they focus the softness of the petals into the centre of the flower.
The ovals may then be filled in with yellow to complete the poinsettia.

Cyclamen

A wild variety of cyclamen makes an interesting study in brush techniques. The flower, with its pale pink blooms, is formed using the same basic petal strokes as the poinsettia. The order of painting is as follows:

This plant has a fat succulent leaf which can best be painted with a large brush loaded with dark blue. If the brush still contains some pink from the flowers, do not wash it all out; the colours will merge giving shading effects. If the dark blue has a touch of watered black, this also adds to the colour interest. Using the full length of the bristles, the brush point remains in one spot, while the bristles are rotated to form the leaf. If a large brush is not available, then this succulent leaf shape can be achieved by constructing two joining leaf shapes. A slight overlap is not unsightly, nor is a slight white space if it results naturally from the stroke structure.

The leaves should grow near the flowers, rich in their profusion. Before the leaves are completely dry, add the veins, using the point of the brush loaded with black ink directly from the ink stone. Keep the pressure light and the veins will be firm without looking hard and dry. All veins start from the same growing point and curve gently to give the leaf shape.

Direction change at the leaf centre

No direction change

Veins closer together on one section of the leaf give the impression of more solid thickness

Addition of the stems allows, in the case of the cyclamen, for some artistic licence, as botanically each leaf and each flowers has a stem of its own. This would make for great overcrowding in a painting, so give stems to only the flowers and buds, painted from the area of growth upwards. The composition can be drastically affected by the positioning of these stems, so care and prior thought are essential.

The final touches to the composition are provided by the stamens and pollen dots. A fine brush, loaded with a dark pink or red, is lightly flicked upwards for each stamen, after the flower is totally dry. These stamens then appear to stand away from the flower because of their clean, hard lines in contrast to the softness of the petals. A few pollen dots should be added for each flower, painted with the soft wet tip of a fine or medium brush, with just enough pressure for the dot to be soft and round. Those dots represent pollen grains and are as different from grains of pepper, salt or sand as chalk from cheese, so be careful with these final touches – not too large, nor too small, but just right for the size of the flower.

Brush Loading with Two or More Colours

One of the most effective techniques produced by the use of the specialised Chinese brush is that of double brush loading. You will also find it useful in any type of water colour painting as well as in pottery decoration.

It is best to use a medium or large brush, in which the bristles are packed quite thickly. A 'rose brush' is a special Chinese brush with shorter-length bristles used for the petals of the peony rose. This can also be double loaded, but it is not suitable for the distribution of three colours.

First make sure that the water colours to be used are ready mixed with water as though to be loaded on to the brush in the usual Chinese manner. For two-colour strokes, load the brush with the lighter of the two colours and then gently scrape the top section of the brush on the side of the palette so that this section is lightly loaded only. Now finish the loading by rolling the brush tip in a darker colour. Practise, using two very different shades of black on the brush so that the technique can easily be seen, but in reality it is better not to have too much contrast between the colours.

Three colours can be loaded on to a Chinese brush, the tip being loaded with the third and darkest colour. The areas where the colours merge into each other produce a very natural effect.

Suitable uses for these effects are in leaves in colour combinations of green and brown as seen in the colour plate 'Chrysanthemums', and in flower petals, either intentionally or even accidentally (see colour plate 'Roses', p. 76).

Monochrome pictures should also have variations of grey and black loaded on to the brush so that in effect light and shade are contained in each stroke.

As many strokes as possible should be painted from one brush loading. Then the brush must be completely emptied of paint and loaded again from the beginning.

Not all the leaves or petals need to be multi-coloured –
the occasional plain one will help set off the complexity of
the shaded ones.

Under no circumstances should colour be added to the
basic stroke in an attempt to achieve shading. Over-
painting or corrections will spoil the free, impressionistic
fluidity of the Chinese brush strokes, so any such
temptation must be firmly resisted. As with all aspects of
Chinese painting techniques, practice is the key to success.

Grapes

Iris

The modern iris has been highly developed and its varieties are colourful and decorative. From the painting point of view the simple wild iris, rather similar to an orchid, is the best type to use as practice.

Using a medium brush, loaded with pale blue water colour (blue and Chinese white combined), the flower is constructed using the basic petal stroke.

Dots or decorative lines can be added to the flower while it is still wet, and yellow pollen dots can be painted on with the tip of the brush.

After painting several flowers and buds, the brush has to be loaded for the leaves. As the leaf is long and thin, the brush must contain sufficient colour (possibly a mixture of grey/green or brown/green) to be able to complete the entire leaf in one stroke, but an over-saturated brush will cause running or unwanted thickness.

Pull the brush firmly but gently over the paper until the end of the envisaged leaf is required and then lift the brush from the paper so that the tip leaves the paper last. If the leaf is to bend, then pull the brush in the direction necessary.

Faults to avoid:

1 Leaf ending is split, not pointed.
 (Cause – lift-off not smooth.)

2 Parallel leaves.

3 Leaves crossing over the top of others.

4 Leaves growing from a base area which is too scattered.

5 All leaves the same length and width.

6 Leaves too similar in colour to each other.

7 Composition spreading out too much.
 (Cause – leaves bending outwards too far.)

8 Proportion of leaf size to flower size incorrect.

9 Composition too crowded.

It may seem, reading this large list of possible faults, that the iris is an extremely difficult flower to paint. This is not so. Practice will show immediate improvement and, if you consider each fault, you will find that most of them can be avoided. Long thin leaves such as these are very elegant as pottery decoration and are later developed further when you come to paint orchid leaves. After thin lines (drawn with a lightly loaded brush held vertically) have been painted from the growing flower clump to each individual iris or bud, the painting is finished – unless you wish to add black vein lines to the leaves. These lines are optional and, in fact, change the painting from a delicate design to a much more positive composition. The lines can be added continuously or in dotted form (much more difficult) and can be arranged to give the leaves a more twisted appearance. It is not advisable to be too careful with these lines or the composition will appear very contrived.

The iris is well worth a great deal of practice as both flowers and leaves are the basis of other stroke constructions.

Plaintain

This is a blue flower with five petals. To the inexperienced artist, the problem of arranging these five petals to fit into a circular format may seem overwhelmingly difficult. However, there is a simple method of approach which can help make this task much easier. An imaginary line is drawn through the centre of the flower and the flower is then arranged with three petals on one side of the line and two petals on the other.

The brush loading for this flower is very important as the stroke requires that the point of the brush remains on the paper while the rest of the bristles rotate until the petal is completed.

Beginning the next stroke close to the previous one, but not touching, lay the brush on the paper and move gently, but positively, anticlockwise. The fourth and fifth petals are completed in a similar manner. The composition requires several flowers in groups, some half hidden by other blooms.

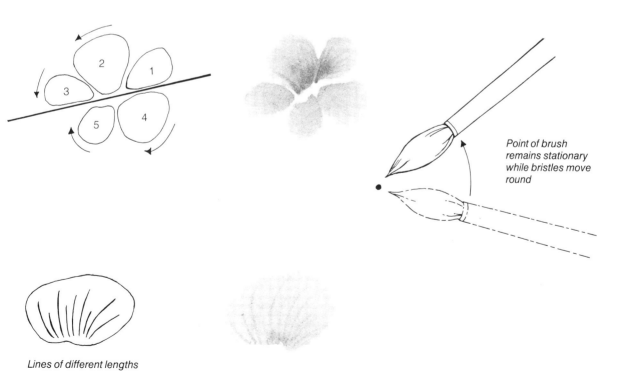

Point of brush remains stationary while bristles move round

Lines of different lengths

While the flowers are still damp, the thin brush, tip loaded with dark blue, inscribes shaping lines to give movement and depth. A long gently curving stamen strikes out from between the petals. Now add orange/yellow pollen dots, scattering them gently around the end of the elongated stamen. Place a few yellow dots in the centre of the flower using a medium brush. There is a temptation here to use the water colour paint too thickly – resist this or it will cause running problems during the mounting process. The leaves lash out from the flowers in straight pale green swathes. Pull the brush along, with a straight lift-off which will give a stubby, rounded end. Variable lengths of leaves and careful direction produce a 'sunburst of green'. One vein line runs through the centre of each leaf.

Paint a thick woody branch appearing from the back of the flower group. This branch is achieved by a push stroke made with a medium brush thickly loaded with dark ink. Very interesting bent branches are the result of pauses and changes of direction during the push stroke. Many of the impressionistic flower compositions have a very positive design content, and this particular grouping is effective both in colour and in various shades of black.

The Outline
Painting Method

There are two methods of painting flowers, the one stroke method and the outline method. The one stroke method of appoach has already been used for both the flowers and the leaves of the poinsettia, cyclamen, iris and plantain. The alternative outline method, although it can be used for both flowers and leaves in one picture, is normally employed for *either* the flowers *or* the leaves in one painting. In essence it can be compared to drawing with a brush, although this is not strictly accurate as the brush movement and direction affect the thickness of the stroke. Brush loading for painting outlines is different from that used to paint leaves and petals as, obviously, only the tip of the brush needs to be loaded. For the beginner it is easier to use thick, black ink directly from the ink stone.

Great care should be taken not to exert too much pressure on the brush when producing these lines – brush pressure causes the ink to be pushed into the paper and this can result in thick lines.

A light touch along the surface will enable you to produce finer lines.

Chrysanthemum

This flower is so important to the Chinese people that it is regarded as one of the 'Four Gentlemen of Chinese Painting'. The chrysanthemum, together with the bamboo, the plum and the orchid, embodies the virtues of strength and beauty even in adversity. Since the T'ang dynasty in AD 618, this flower which blossoms in spite of the wind and the frost in the difficult autumn season, has become instantly recognised as an embodiment of the simple oriental art form.

Since it is not customary in China to paint with the flower as a living model, the form and characteristics of each individual type must be known. The artist has both to study and to love the chrysanthemum in order to be able to convey readily his remembered impressions on to paper. This method of 'mind painting' has both advantages and disadvantages. On the credit side, one is not sidetracked or distracted by the necessity to match colour shades exactly, or be dominated by the direction and intensity of the light. Flaws are no longer remembered so do not have to be recorded, which can only be an advantage. However, it is necessary to develop a high degree of observation and interest and a very selective colour sense. The peculiarities of this system of painting account for several facets of Chinese painting: the tendency of artists to specialise in very specific subjects e.g. horses, monkeys, prawns, bamboo etc., and also the great length of time which elapses before an oriental person considers himself to be artistically competent in one particular branch of painting.

Our modern hustle and bustle must be abandoned for a slower more natural life style if success is to come in the field of Chinese painting. Careful study of the flowers as they change with the seasons leads to an appreciation of the continuing pattern of nature and a fascinating new awareness of the beauty of the chrysanthemum. This type of study in depth will be helpful in all flower painting as one becomes aware of the particular characteristics of each flower.

A chrysanthemum flower is made up of many petals radiating out from the centre and spread out in circles which eventually build up to form the full flower head.

As the petals are added stroke by stroke, the flower grows before your eyes. Using the outline method, start from the centre of the flower and paint each petal in two strokes. A fine brush loaded with dark ink directly from the ink stone is the best way to begin. It is necessary to load only the tip of the brush since it is a fine line which is required.

Make the petals slightly different until the circle is completed.

Add more petals in between the first layer.

Buds can also be constructed in the same way.

Flowers and buds are arranged together in groups of three or five, depending upon the size of the flowers. (See colour plate of 'Chrysanthemums'.) Next in the designated order of painting are the leaves. Chrysanthemum leaves are either three-lobed or five-lobed. Remember that nature is rarely perfectly symmetrical, so if each section of the leaf is slightly different in size and shape the overall result will be better than if each lobe is exactly the same. When all the leaves have been added, the main stems are placed carefully, using the basic 'push stroke'. Then each unattached leaf is joined to the stem, always painting *from* the central leaf vein *to* the main stem. This chrysanthemum picture can be left as a monochrome picture, or the outlines can be filled in with colour. Any colour can be used, or even two if desired, but the water colour must be gently delicate in shade, not thick and heavy. Fill in the spaces rather roughly so that parts of the white paper still show through, and a very realistic flower will result.

Each type of chrysanthemum has different characteristics. Some are flat with thin petals, some are small and round with tightly packed petals, and others have delicately flowing curving petals, while the shape of the flower head can vary from dome-shaped to disc-shaped. Another type of chrysanthemum which lends itself to this type of painting is the spider variety. Thinner longer petals point upwards to the sky and elegant spiderish petals weave their way downwards, interlacing as they go. The most difficult area in the construction of these flowers is the centre. Be careful not to form a darkened area where too much painting has overlapped.

A favourite type of composition is one which combines chrysanthemums with rock, as the gentle softness of the flower is thrown into high relief by the dark strength of the rock structure.

Hydrangea

The hydrangea consists of small four-petalled flowers. These small flowers group together to form a large flower head whose colours of pink, blue or lavender make a very fine and colourful display. Either flower painting method can be used for these flowers, with the rather large leaves which frame the flower head being painted in the 'one-stroke' technique.

The flowers cluster together naturally in such a way that occasionally not all the four petals are on view at the same time. Think of the flower as growing from a centre outwards and build up the florets accordingly. The final shape should be relatively round, but not circular. One of the problems to avoid is that concentration on the actual strokes can be so intense that, before you realise it, the flower may grow out of all proportion into a monster of the giant sunflower type. A fine brush, loaded with dark ink directly from the ink stone, is the easiest method of outlining the florets, although it is also possible to use a lighter shade of black, or even a colour for the flower heads.

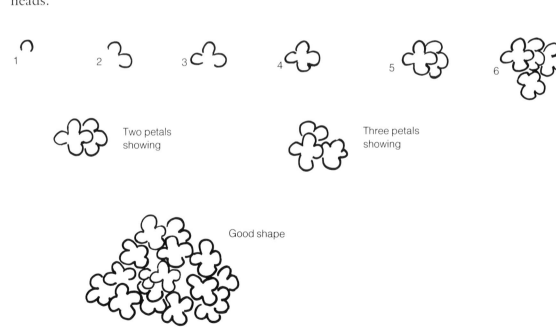

1

2

3

4

5

6

Two petals showing

Three petals showing

Good shape

Usually more than one flower is necessary for a good composition. Each should be different in size and shape from the other, but if unsure, then always place the heaviest, largest flower towards the bottom of the group. The flower heads should all be very close together. The next stage is to add leaves, beginning near the flower heads. Each leaf is a simple basic stroke framing the flower. The first leaves should begin as close to the flower head as possible without actually being allowed to touch it. Remember not to paint one leaf over the top of another, but stop and start again on the other side of the leaf.

The stems should not be too long as the intention is to suggest a small group of flowers from a large bush. Paint from the bottom of the stem towards the flower, stopping where leaves cross the path of brush movement.

Once again it becomes evident that to achieve simplicity requires care and attention to detail and also continuous concentration from the beginning of the end of the painting.

Orchid

Chueh Yin, a Buddhist monk of the Yuan period, suggested that the painter in a happy mood should paint the orchid because 'the leaves grow as though they are flying and fluttering and the buds open joyfully'.

The most difficult part in painting the orchid is the achievement of the long leaf strokes; so, unlike other flower painting compositions, the leaves are painted first. The grass orchid species which has only one flower on each stalk is called 'lan' and its leaves grow in tufts of not more than seven, while several orchids on one stem, the marsh orchid, known as 'hui', has leaf clumps of not more than eleven blades.

There is a special order of painting for the leaves:

1 The first stroke in an arc.

2 The second stroke crosses forming the 'phoenix eye'.

3 The third blade goes between to 'break the eye'.

Others are then added.

The leaves should be darker than the flowers and not all of the same length. Sometimes a break may occur in the stroke; this does not matter and in fact illustrates the Chinese principle that there is continuity of idea, even if a break in its execution occurs. (The Chinese description of this is rather clever – 'idea present, brush absent'.)

The orchid can be painted growing from a rock, or near a brook, or just growing from the ground, but the leaves must be graceful and curved, almost, in fact, a complete composition in their own right.

Orchid flowers are usually lighter in colour and tone than the leaves, and the flower petals should have dark tips to them. The five-petalled flower should not be painted like an outstretched hand, but like fingers with one or two curled across each other and some straight. The larger petals are straight and broad, while the smaller, narrower ones curl. The stamens, the heart of the flower, are painted like three dots and vary in position according to the direction in which the orchid flower itself faces.

The orchid is one of the 'Four Gentlemen of Chinese Painting' and those who look at the work of the ancient masters can see why it is said that 'the brush dances and the ink sings'.

Marsh Orchid

Plum Blossom

Another one of the 'Four Gentlemen of Chinese Painting' is the plum, the others being orchid, bamboo and chrysanthemum. Each of these different living plant forms represents characteristics regarded by the Chinese scholar as worthy of emulation.

Plum blossom in its different stages of growth, together with its developing trunk and subsidiary branches, represents the continuity of life. The delicate flowering blooms appear to be at one with the January frost, symbolising hope and endurance. It is not customary to devote an entire composition to one tree, but to show, by means of a small group of branches, a microcosm of its entire existence. A twisted, gnarled trunk bears slim, elegant branches, which in their turn sprout young shoots, buds and blossoms in all their many aspects.

*Examples of flowers
(out-line technique)*

Time is crystallised, encapsulated into an evocative composition in which a few lines and simple strokes tell all. Nowhere is the ideal of space, which is so much a part of Chinese painting, more beneficially shown than in a plum blossom composition. The space is integral to the design iself. At any moment buds may open filling one space, while another dies and falls to the ground, leaving its scent lingering in the void which will be left. Yang and Yin, the Chinese concepts so basic to its painting, is epitomised here. Dark, heavy, old twisted trunk, contrasting with light, young straight shoots; the soft roundness of the blossom enhancing the straight hardness of the branch. Symbolically, the plum is regarded as having two trunks, one large and one small, with the bud representing Heaven and Earth in a form undivided by the appearance of Man.

The main branches symbolise the four seasons and tend to face in towards the four direction of the Universe. It is a tree with dignity.

Simple blossom. (Notice the space left in the branches for the flowers.)

Blossom and bamboo in the moonlight.
(The moon is achieved by painting with a large brush
around a circular object.)

Instructions for painting the plum are almost poetic. Fresh tips of branches are luxuriantly covered in blossom, the flowers and buds being small in proportion to the thickness of the trunk or branch. Where branches connect or fork, they mingle busily together. Branches do not grow in opposite directions from the same point on the trunk. It is customary when painting this subject to paint the branches first, leaving spaces for the blossoms to be inserted later. This calls for a very clear concept of the composition as a whole before you start. It is not an easy subject to capture, but it is always worth the effort.

The blossoms can be formed in many ways, wide open or about to drop, fully formed or merely buds; there is no limit to their variety. The form of the blossom has been compared to the 'eyes of the crab', 'grains of pepper' or sometimes 'like a smile'. Blossom should be soft and round and grow from its heart, which the Chinese compare to the hole in the centre of a coin.

Plum blossom can be painted either in the outline technique or with solid strokes, but in both cases life is given to the flower by the addition of the anthers, stamens and pistil. Stamens should be 'as strong as the whiskers of a tiger' says the basic Chinese instruction book and the anthers dotted 'like grains of pepper' or 'the eyes of crabs'.

Other blossom is composed in a similar way, but none are quite as striking to the 'Chinese eye' as the purity and strength of plum blossom.

Autumn

Landscape Painting

Landscape always has been, and still is, the great subject of Chinese painting. Mountains were not only the magical abode of spirits, but also the centre of the four directions of the Universe. Nature pervades everything, but the Chinese landscape is composed of symbols or ideal types. Thus there is a specific method of painting the elm-type tree, willow or pine. It is not possible in reality to 'copy' nature, therefore the intention is to 'create' a landscape painting. This creation can best be described as an aristocratic production.

The simple landscape opposite, basically trees and rocks, has been painted with very wet brush strokes. Each stroke is made by placing the brush length sideways on to the paper and allowing the wet black ink to run.

Mountains

The basic overall structure is the most important idea to bear in mind when starting to paint a landscape, particularly a large one. The ancient Chinese painters divided their space into three or four main sections and then worked from there, first establishing the general outlines of the mountains. The later details and individual changes of brush strokes can be worked out when the whole composition has been planned.

The great master painters of the past had a saying, 'yu pi yu mo', which means 'to have brush, to have ink' and implies that outline without the brush strokes that give it depth is as bad as having the solidity of the ink strokes without the clarity of the outline. Both these requirements are necessary parts of the effective whole. Usually it is the crowning peak which is the dominant overall mountain; others are added, sometimes in a subservient position, and at other times side by side as though friends. Too many peaks will not make a successful painting as the effect will be dull and monotonous. Mountains are often described as being in a 'host-guest' relationship – in fact these friendly groupings are an integral part of rock and tree groupings as well as mountain arrangements.

Rocks

From ancient times the Chinese have regarded rocks and stones as more than mere geological matter. The medicinal qualities of their mineral ingredients have given rocks a magical connotation. Rock is the backbone of the earth and the element which gives it its strength. As it comes in so many forms, it can be interpreted in a variety of decorative ways, all of them involved with the basic Yin–Yang principle so inherent in landscape painting. A quotation from Tsung Ping sums up the Chinese idea as follows: 'Landscape paintings have a material existence and also a spiritual influence.'

To the Chinese it is essential that even a rock has a spirit of its own; this quality is as basic as their formation and the Chinese call it 'ch'i'. The first outlining of the rock should have life, otherwise everything that follows can be worthless.

Light ink places and outlines the rock and then the modelling brush strokes follow to give the rock its three faces. Either dots or lines to represent the veins are placed inside the outline until the rock emerges as a living form. The side of the brush is used for rocks whose moulding lines are straight, while the point is the vital part of the brush for rocks whose modelling lines are like 'tangled hemp fibres'. Picturesque descriptions for the methods of delineating rocks abound: Fan K'uan used 'ravelled rope' strokes; Ma Yuan's strokes were like 'brushwood in disorder'; Hsia Kuei described his brush strokes as 'big axe cuts' and Wang Wei as 'veins of a lotus leaf'.

How to Paint Rocks

Using the lightest possible tone of black ink in the beginning and a featherlight touch on the paper, draw the point of the brush up to the top of the rock and then continuously lay the bristles down and gently pull to the right. Then push horizontally to the left. (This description is for right-handed people. If you are left-handed you should reverse all the instructions.) Step by step darker tones can be added. Each brush stroke should move and turn with abrupt stops as this gives angularity and volume to the rock.

Small rocks can build up into large mountains by indicating the outlines and then adding crevices and hollows. For clouds and mists washes should be soft and light among the mountains.

When planning a picture, first work out the proportions of the sky and earth; the top half is sky space, the bottom half is earth space and in between are organised the details of the landscape.

A Chinese saying goes 'Learn from the teacher, but avoid his limitations'. Eventually each painter will develop a rock painting method which will give life and form to the rocks of his landscape picture.

A painting of clouds and mist

This painting shows how small rocks build up into groups, then grow into mountains

Holiday Island

The Four Chief Stages in Landscape Painting

The four chief stages in landscape painting are outlines, shaping lines, dots and washes.

1 Outlines

Outlines can be superimposed over each other in several layers of ink, usually lighter ink first, although it is possible for the really expert painter to work the other way round. Changes and corrections can be made as layers build up from light to dark. The effect is more subtle and less committed when the outlines are painted in this order.

2 Shaping lines

There are outlines for rocks, mountains and trees made up of 'shaping lines' which meld together to form the landscape and which give it its style. These lines can be compared to handwriting, in that, even when trying very carefully to achieve a certain style of shaping line, the result is dominated by the painter's own personality traits. It becomes impossible to efface individuality even when trying exceptionally hard to achieve a specific type of modelling line.

Three main categories of line have been loosely defined, each with their own picturesque description of the minor varieties. *Thread-shaped lines* can be described as veins of lotus leaves, hemp fibres, cow hair, whirlpool eddies or lumps of alum; while the *band-shaped lines* are like axe-cuts of different sizes or horses' teeth. The third category, *dot-shaped lines*, can be like thorns or raindrops or the ubiquitous 'mi dots'. However, a painter eventually develops his own types of shaping lines, instinctively choosing the type which will best describe the intentions of his painting.

Although the basic shaping lines are clearly defined, they can be made to appear totally different as variable factors, such as the dryness of the brush, the angle at which the brush is held and the pressure and speed of the brush movements, are taken into consideration.

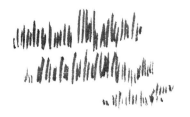

Various types of shaping lines

Brush movements. Use a small brush, lightly loaded. The brush moves in the direction of the arrows and in the order shown.

More shaping lines

Work from very light centre line. Use small brush, with medium ink loading.

Rather wetter brush, placed on the paper with a sideways movement, allowing some ink to run.

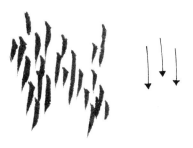

Foliage shaping lines

Small brush, held vertically over the paper, with medium loading. Brush not to move too slowly.
Stroke starts at the top and brush moves down.

Brush moves from the outside towards the centre, eventually completing a full circle.

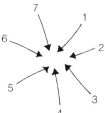

Brush to be loaded with rather more ink, and moved slightly more slowly, but still as above.

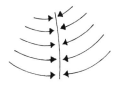

Begin with centre line. Then work from the outside inwards.

More landscape shaping strokes

Use medium brush with medium loading.

Remember to vary the shades of ink used to paint these shaping lines, although to begin with it is always easier to paint with thick ink.

Brush laid down horizontally, point to the left.

Brush held vertically, allowed to touch the paper.

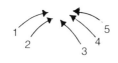

Rapid brush strokes, forming a fan shape, with movements from the outside towards the centre.

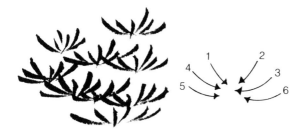

Fan shape formed by brush strokes made in the order shown.

3 Dots

After the basic structure of the landscape painting has been clearly delineated, any necessary dots can now be added. These serve to emphasise any lines which need to be strengthened or can be used to remove the impression of over-smoothness of tree trunks or rocks. Although dots, like lines, have tendencies towards the horizontal, vertical or diagonal, they can be varied by different brush usage and even superimposed on each other in variable ink strengths. There are many different kinds of ink dots in the same way as there are myriad varieties of grains like pepper, salt, sand or pollen; some are soft and should be painted with loose wet ink; others are hard and best expressed with a dry brush.

Dots can be used to emphasise the folds of the hills or to show distant vegetation; or put together in varying combinations to indicate other elements of the landscape.

4 Washes

Sometimes a landscape painting will not require any wash, either in ink or colour, but usually some form of space filling is required. There are two types of wash which may be used, although they are often painted in conjunction with each other. Small areas of wash, for instance, on rocks or foreground can help to give added perspective to the composition. An overall wash on large areas of painting is called 'jan'. It is very important to keep this wash even and not to use too heavy a colour. It is also customary to put an overall wash on top of the smaller areas which have already been painted so it is vital neither to over-soak the paper with liquid, nor to scrape the surface of the paper when applying paint to large areas. Occasionally when using very white paper for landscape painting, it may improve the composition to cover the entire landscape with a wash of tea, thus giving a ready-made ageing effect to the painting. Tea is, after all, a natural stain and practice and experience can determine the degree of concentration required to attain the exact colour needed. Once again, care must be taken not to scrape the paper surface or tear it when it is vulnerably wet.

Chinese landscape painting is called 'shan-shui hua' which means 'the painting of mountains and water'. It also embodies the Yin–Yang principle which underlies Chinese philosophy. The male element, Yang, is the mountain and the female element, Yin, is the water. Water is the weakest element in the universe, but by continuous soft pressure it penetrates and weakens the hardest of substances, like rock, so that eventual erosion is inevitable. Water is rarely the main element of a Chinese landscape painting, but it is almost always there – implied if not actually seen and all-pervasive in its presence. It is not delineated by small elegantly described rivulets and waves, but by space in the foreground, waterfalls hiding at the back, or snow lying gently on the hills.

Use of Colour

Ink is always the central core of Chinese painting, but colour can help to provide more realism. All the ink strokes should be completed first before any colour is added, though it may in fact be the case that a particular composition stands in its own right without the need of any colour at all. Otherwise the use of water colours, which are, of course, transparent, will give the picture additional realism while allowing the brush strokes, the essence of Chinese painting, to show through.

One of the difficulties which has occurred as a result of modern progressive developments is that water colours are no longer pure pigments, but contain additives which help to maintain free-flowing qualities in the paint, or alternatively keep the colour intensity fast under difficult light conditions. These very advances cause difficulties to the modern Chinese painter as some of the twentieth-century man-made 'improvements' do not, in fact, meld with the ink and rice paper in the same way as the original pigments.

The Poet

Perspective

On a two-dimensional surface the appearance of three-dimensional space can only be an illusion. The ability of the painter to convey this illusion is the essence of landscape painting. The Chinese use two methods: first, by making the objects diminish in size the further back they are and second, by making distant objects indistinct and painting them in a paler colour.

There is no focal point in a Chinese landscape; it is all open to be viewed from any position, but the painter himself keeps a persistent position which falls into one of the three main categories allowed for the landscape artist.

1 *High Distance* (kao yuan)

Looking at a peak from the bottom upwards. This gives a precipitous view as the eye moves from the base of the picture upwards.

High distance (kao yuan)

2 *Deep Distance* (shen yuan)

Looking across from a foreground mountain to one at the back of the picture to give the effect of many different layers to be viewed as the eye travels from front to back.

Deep distance (shen yuan)

3 Level Distance (p'ing yuan)

Looking from a place in the foreground into the far
distance across a flat landscape. The eye can encompass the
entire view calmly and without much eye movement.

Level distance (p'ing yuan)

Kuo Hsi, in the early part of the eleventh century, added these comments to help clarify the three types of landscape painting. In high perspective, everything appears bright and clear with human figures quite definite; in deep perspective, objects are deep and heavy with human figures appearing to be broken up; while in the third category, there are shadings which are light and shadowy with figures appearing in very soft focus.

Specific sizes are important too. The mountain is bigger than the trees and the trees are bigger than the men. In fact Taoist philosophy almost demands that the size of man should be underemphasised to give it its correct importance in the overall plan of nature – people being regarded as of very small significance in the general order of things. Kuo Hsi also said 'In landscape, paint mountains in tens of feet, trees in feet, horses in inches and humans in tenths of an inch'.

Additional elements can be introduced into the landscape painting to add extra emphasis to each different type of perspective structure. Mountains can be made to appear higher by the addition of waterfalls, or huts nestling at different levels on the hills. Mists and variable breaks in the many planes which make up the landscape in depth can help to extend the distance, while flowers and birds in the foreground of a level perspective landscape maintain differential interests.

Drawing Trees

There is an accepted order for drawing trees as there is for all parts of the Chinese landscape. First the trunk is drawn, then the main branches, followed by the foliage. Branches fork out like roads and paths. Two trees together are composed either as a large tree with a small tree added (called 'fu lao' meaning carrying the old on the back) or if painted the other way round, then it is regarded as 'hsieh yu' (leading the young by the hand). Trees should not all be the same height but should appear to be growing naturally together.

Pine Trees

Pine trees are very important to the Chinese landscape painter, not only to the actual composition of the picture itself, but also because the tree represents so many fine virtues and high principles. Its inner strength symbolises the inner virtues of man, the potential which is available ready to be tapped. The tree itself is often compared to a dragon, a symbol of power, either lean and strong, coiled ready to emerge, or old and sturdy and as strong as iron. Anyone visiting a pinetum will realise just how many variations there are of the pine tree. Observation always helps, but simple decorative elegance and careful brush strokes produce extraordinary results. Trees in the foreground of the landscape have a great deal of detail you can show, remembering always that it must be in correct proportion to the overall composition; while those in the background have progressively less detail, culminating in a series of vertical lines with small horizontal 'rice' strokes to indicate distant pines.

One individual branch is sometimes used as a complete composition in its own right, in which case each needle assumes very great importance. The size, and number, of needles per group has to be varied according to the general size of the pine tree composition.

When looking at pine trees as part of a larger landscape the general impression is often of fan-shaped areas of green or grey through which the needles shine. To represent this, the needles are drawn first with the brush and then soft wet brush strokes provide the overall softening effect.

Simple method of painting pine trees

pine needles   shape

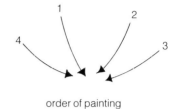

order of painting

group shape

needles in group shape

grey small wash added

several groups of pine
needles with wash added

*Long-needled pine tree
in very simple form*

A tree painted in two different styles

Other Landscape Trees

Many other trees figure quite largely in the general landscape composition, as the tree cult has symbolised life and death from very early times. Hollow trees were regarded as being filled with spirit and were particularly significant. ('Spirit' here implies life feeling.) The mulberry tree has roots reaching into the nether regions and branches ascending to the sky above; the sun climbs it every day according to ancient mythology. The cassia is the tree of the night and darkness, and its flowers are described as 'luminous stars lighting the world before sunrise'. All manuals on Chinese brush painting describe the Wu Tung tree (dryandra) since it is associated with the legendary phoenix. The willow tree, always associated with and usually painted with water, is a favourite tree in a small landscape composition and much appreciated by the Western admirer of Chinese art. There are several methods of painting the foliage: one is to outline the leaves and fill them in with green; another is to paint the leaves directly in yellow green in the single-stroke technique or, of course, ink monochrome can be used with great subtlety to achieve the same results.

Ducks and willow

Two types of palm tree in outline technique

Various kinds of distant foliage

Waterfalls

Some form of water is almost an essential in a true traditional landscape painting. Water is the life blood of nature, but even more important, it gives life and vitality to the rather static form of landscape which is so favoured by the Chinese painter.

It can be said that while rocks form the basic structure of mountains and therefore landscape painting, water forms the rocks and the mountains.

A waterfall may be shown as a small, gently flowing water way or as a powerful substance which has cut through a steep mountain gorge. Wang Wei described the painting of a waterfall as an idea having 'interruptions, but no breaks'; in other words, the brush may stop but the thought continues. One device which was often used was to have clouds partly obscuring the waterfall, so that some of the flow is implied rather than actually seen.

On no account should water appear from nowhere in an impossible manner as this would immediately render the landscape painting worthless.

People and Things

Landscape painting does not have to have people and things in it, but they are often a useful means of conveying size.

Figures are usually drawn carefully with a fine brush, but not in too much detail. Figures should be kept in proportion to the trees as far as possible, but should on no account be painted larger than a mountain even if normal non-oriental rules of perspective seem to require it. Man, to the Chinese landscape painter, is a very insignificant part of the overall conception and as such should be shown by his size to be so.

The viewer of a landscape painting should want to change places with the person in the painting. A figure contemplating the mountain or playing a musical instrument, or a philosopher relaxing by a mountain stream; all these contribute to the overall composition without distracting from the scenic beauty.

In some cases, although it is obvious what the people are doing, they may be drawn so freely that they have no eyes or ears or other fine detail. Still, they contribute to the general effect without impinging too much on the peaceful aspect of the Chinese landscape. Animals and birds, although they may seem to be only a very small part of the landscape painting, are in reality playing a large part as they are helping to convey the season or the time of day. They also help to give a feeling of life and some vitality to a rather stationary art form.

Houses

Usually a landscape will contain some kind of dwelling. The Chinese regard the doors and windows of these dwellings in the same way as eyes and eyebrows; it is where they are placed which is important and how they are positioned. Without them the house is 'blind', but with too many doors and windows, the house would become ridiculous. Landscapes acquire life from both dwellings and people, but if overpopulated the peace and tranquillity of the painting could be ruined.

Buildings rising on the levels of a mountain slope.

Thatched dwellings. These can be used in summer landscapes, sometimes with open windows, or occasionally with the windows closed up.

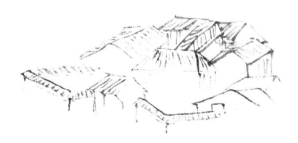

Houses suitable for flat areas.

A hut and its gate – a natural scene filled with life. It can be used in landscapes – in rain or in snow. A vine grows untidily across the gateway as this small cameo conjures up visions rather than carefully explaining facts.

The Twelve Faults as Listed by Jao Tzu-jan

These are the faults to be avoided in landscape painting and indeed, if all these errors could be averted, then the painting would be well on its way to being a work of art:

1   A crowded, ill-arranged composition.

2   Far and near not clear.

3   Mountains without life.

4   Water with no source.

5   Over-simplified landscapes.

6   Paths with no beginning or end.

7   Stones and rocks with one face.

8   Trees with less than four main branches.

9   Unnatural figures.

10   Buildings in the wrong place.

11   Mixed atmospheric effects.

12   Colour applied without thought.

If this list is studied carefully, it becomes clear that most of these faults have already been mentioned in the course of each individual description of the different parts of landscape painting which fit together to make the whole. However, while it is easy to remember when one is only concerned with one aspect at a time, it is much more difficult to maintain the level of concentration required to ensure that not a single one of these mistakes creeps into an entire painting. One small consolation, if such it be, is that it is obvious from the list that even the best of the ancient Chinese painters was not immune from making the odd mistake, otherwise there would clearly not have been any need for this list.

The Seal or Chop

When or who started the practice of appending a seal to a painting or work of art is rather obscure, but without doubt it is of the utmost importance.

The first seal placed by the artist shows its authenticity and may be followed by another different one, possibly to depict another facet of the artist, in the form of a nom-de-plume or artistic symbol. These two almost certainly would be of the basic two types: one with the characters on the seal carved in relief, giving red characters on a white ground with a red border, cameo form, and the other being carved to produce white characters with a red background, intaglio form – yet another oriental preoccupation with Yin and Yang. Many seals are themselves works of art and, if made in ivory or jade, greatly prized.

Owners of paintings or their friends would possibly add their own chop, partly to show their approval, but also to give a visible record of the pedigree of the painting, who owned it and when. The owner or collector could also add a written dedication (a colophon) to any painting he liked, but these frequently became cumbersome or ill-placed and destroyed the basic beauty of the orignal painting.

A good seal colour will not run or fade for hundreds of years, but needless to say the quality of the ink may vary and can be an expensive item. It is a very thick sticky red paste made of cinnabar (mercuric oxide) which gives the red colour, oils and shredded raw silk and to use it properly requires practice and patience. The seal is pressed into the ink a few times and is then transferred on to the painting, making sure that firm even pressure is applied to gain an imprint which will remain legible for a considerable period of time.

Opposite: a selection of authentic chops ranging from the twelfth century to the twentieth century

Chrysanthemums.
Painted on silk

How to Make Your Chop

Ideally your own name translated into Chinese characters would be most suitable, but very few European or Occidental names translate effectively enough into Chinese to make this worthwhile. As a compromise, therefore, you could use the initials of your name to experiment with. Use them either as they are (e.g. ABC) or as a concocted 'Chinese-looking' anagram. This is actually not for the purist or faint-hearted. So, ABC could become

(twice size)

as JL into

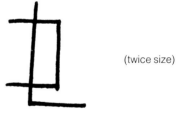

(twice size)

Simplicity is the key to successful chop design in this way.

If on the other hand you are a flower painter or prefer birds etc. then a simple motif design can be made, but these latter types are only really fully effective when used in conjunction with another using characters of some description.

(twice size)

Whatever design or designs you choose, scale them down to about 1 × ¾ inch (2 × 1.5 cm), draw them reversed and check in a mirror that your reversing has been done correctly.

Transfer this reversed design on to a small piece of hard, fine-grained wood, *bigger than your actual design*, which has been well sanded to a smooth and flat surface. Again check in a mirror that the design is correct.

Now, using a vice to secure the wood firmly, take an engraver or fine carving tool and slowly *either* carve away the design, thus leaving the surround which will be red when used, *or* carve so as to leave the design intact. The latter obviously gives the more effective result, but does take much longer and if you make a mistake or cut anything wrongly is impossible to alter.

Before trimming the block to the final size clean the surface and carved parts. Ensure that the final piece has square corners and straight sides. Other shapes are made, but often look out of place in company with predominantly rectangular ones.

It is sometimes possible to find a piece of flat soft stone, soapstone for instance, with a smooth surface which can be used in much the same way as wood, *but* being more brittle, it is inclined, if extra care is not taken, to splinter and chip. Finally before you use the chop on a painting make sure the block is marked so that it shows which way you should hold it to ensure that it prints the correct way up.

Placing the chop on the finished painting is not difficult, but before the imprint is made, every care should be taken to find the best position, usually at the lower corners or upper corners. The first chop is never placed in the centre of the sides or within the painting itself. It may be considered as only a signature, but as it is very distinctive in colour, any error in its location will be most noticeable and could destroy the overall efficacy of the painting. Never append any other initials or signature and wait until the painting has been trimmed to its final size and shape.

Keep the chop surface clean at all times so that the outlines remain clean and not 'furry' and it goes without saying that the 'ink' is most indelible and every care must be taken to prevent it from being smudged – it does not dry instantaneously and as it is poisonous, it is not advisable to get it in the mouth.

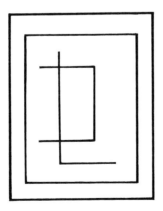

The chop as printed

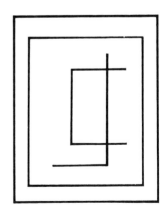

The chop as cut

Hibiscus

Practical
Chinese Painting

The Essence of Chinese Painting

To Western eyes most Chinese paintings seem to be very similar and lacking in originality. In fact, this is true. Chinese painters repeat the same themes over and over again, basing their interpretations on Master painters of the past. However, each interpretation is made original by nuances of difference, which are as clear to the Eastern eye as are the contrasts between Picasso and Rembrandt to the Westerner.

An analogy to music is most appropriate. The same piece of music can be brought to life by a skilful musician, or destroyed by an incompetent one. Chinese painting can be seen as a new interpretation of a well-known composition, brought to fruition by an accomplished artist. As with music, the artist must first master the technicalities of his media before he can achieve a polished interpretation.

The static culture of the Chinese has contributed in no small way to the continuity of traditional styles of painting, most importantly because until the twentieth-century evolution of the fountain pen, and now the ballpoint pen, everyone used a brush for writing and so had the basis of the technical skill which could be developed through calligraphy into painting.

The essence of Chinese painting is derived from nature. Topics such as flowers, birds, landscapes, insects and fish abound. Most paintings are simple in subject matter – a bird sitting on the branch of a tree; an insect poised to alight on a flower. These subjects are not painted outside in the real world but derive from concepts of them held in the artist's mind. A great deal of contemplation of the ever-changing panorama of nature is necessary to achieve such a clear visual picture that, almost without conscious volition, the brush can convey these mind pictures on to the painting surface.

The Western artist usually brings his or her painting subject into the studio to observe in close detail while painting, or sits outside, sketch book in hand, to convey the form on to paper, but the Chinese artist does not work in this way because the object is not to portray a realistic or even a naturalistic image, but to show in symbolic form the essence of the subject.

Flower and bird painting: Parrot and Blossom

Colour

There have been long periods of time during the development of Chinese painting when colour was regarded as superficial and much to be avoided, as philosopher painters searched for calmness and detachment in their painting. The belief that the inner essence and spirit of objects could be rendered more clearly in shades of black, undistracted by colour, was a result of the close alliance of painting to calligraphy.

Philosophers commented adversely on colour in everyday life, Confucius complaining that the purples and mixed reds of the court robes were decadent and Lao Tsu writing in *Tao Te Ching* that 'the Five Colours will blind the eye'.

The Chinese language not only has few words to distinguish specific colours but the written word for colour itself, '*se*', also means beauty, passion, anger and lewdness.

However, nearly half of all Chinese paintings use some colour in addition to black, and some historic painting periods are particularly noted for colour. Before the Sung period, the use of bright colours was quite common, and an early descriptive term for painting was *tan Ch'ing* (the reds and blues). During the T'ang period (AD 618-906), landscapes in blue and green were so popular that this kind of painting has become inextricably linked with thoughts of that time.

Later painters described their compositions as having 'ink and light colour' especially where this applied to small or large colour washes. Flower and bird painters used colour more extensively, particularly if they were employing the 'one-stroke' technique.

Colour Symbolism

Colour symbolism associated the Five Colours with the Five Points of the Compass and the symbolic Chinese creatures which rule the heavens, each of which is associated with a magic number, as well as with the Five Elements, the Five Ch'i (the atmospheric elements) and the Five Planets. The Five Tastes, the Five Organs and the Five Sounds were also connected with corresponding colours.

Chart showing the colour associations

Colour	Compass points	Supernatural creatures	Numbers	Elements	Planets	Seasons	Metal
Black	North	tortoise or snake	6	water	Mercury	winter	iron
Red	South	phoenix	7	fire	Mars	summer	copper
Green	East	blue/green dragon	8	wood	Jupiter	spring	lead
White	West	tiger	9	metal	Venus	autumn	silver
Yellow	Centre	yellow dragon	5	earth	Saturn		gold

Papercuts of stage masks showing different make-ups

Colours can also be symbolic of rank, authority, virtues and vices, joys and sorrows.

Red	joy and all festive occasions, visiting cards
Yellow	the National colour, sacred to the Emperor and his sons
Blue	for high officials' sedan chairs (green for lower officials)
White	for mourning
Black	for evil
Vermilion	for the Emperor's special edicts
Mauve	for seals of the highest authority

In Buddhism, the gods are white, goblins are red and devils are black, while yellow is the colour used for the priestly robes.

The origin of the red paper scrolls which hang in pairs to protect the home is a development of a legend with similarities to the Jewish Passover. Lamb's blood was used to smear the door lintels to represent the New Year sacrifice to Heaven. Charms against evil spirits were written on yellow paper.

Certain colours were used as royal colours for dynasties: Southern Sung (AD 960–1126) was brown; Ming (AD 1368–1644) was green; Ch'ing (AD 1644–1911) was yellow.

In the theatre, stage make-up designated the characters of the players: red for a sacred person, black for honesty, white for a cunning person, though one with dignity, while a low comedian had a white nose only.

The Republican Flag of China had five colours for the five races of China: red for Manchurians, yellow for Chinese, blue for Mongolians, white for Mohammedans and black for Tibetans.

Red paper sign for door. Photo(s) by Xie Jun, Zhou Youma and Huo Jianying

Red and black have always been the most important of the Five Colours as their association is with the Primary Elements of Fire and Water, with Heaven and Earth and with Yang and Yin. They, as with the other three colours, were believed to have magical powers associated with Taoist alchemy. This is not surprising in view of the original methods of pigment preparation, which took place in secrecy with incantations.

Chinese black ink is prepared from pine soot which is then mixed with glue, pressed into moulds and dried to form ink sticks or ink cakes. When it is needed, the ink stick is ground with water on a flat ink stone to make the black ink. The other four colours were originally either of mineral or vegetable origin and were ground in a bowl with water or glue added to reach the required consistency.

Colours from vegetable and mineral sources

Colours	Mineral	Vegetable
blues/greens	azurite, malachite	indigo
reds	iron oxides, orpiment, coral	cinnabar, a red-leaved vine
yellow	iron oxide	sap of the rattan plant
white	lead	crushed oyster or clam shells

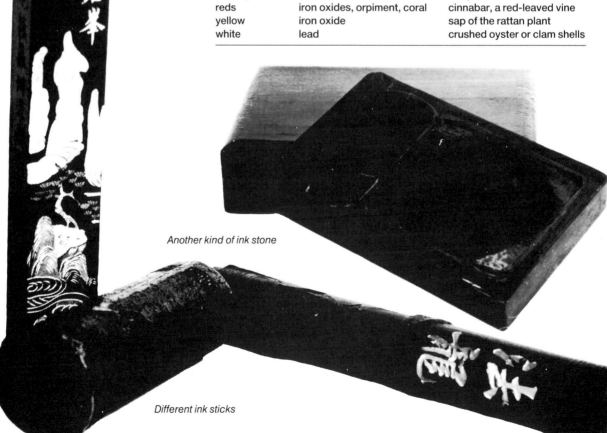

Another kind of ink stone

Different ink sticks

Old manuals give surprising hints for painters in their use of colour. The juice of an apricot seed can be used to wipe painted white clean if it has darkened, they say. Or a little ear wax added to mineral blue or ink which is grainy will help to improve the consistency.

Colour Mixing Chart

Yellow and blue = green
Crimson and blue = purple
Yellow and red = brown

The above are three basic combinations of yellow, blue and red, but the proportions in which these colours are mixed, together with the additional shade combinations available from adding white or black, are described in the following chart:

Table of colour mixing

Colour obtained	Basic colours					
	crimson	vermilion	sky blue/ indigo	white	yellow/ gamboge	black ink
pink	3 parts			7 parts		
gold red	2	2			1	
purple	5		4			
violet	3		6			1
sap green			1		1	
deep green			3		2	
light green			3		7	
inky green			4		3	3
inky blue			7			3
gold yellow	1	2			7	
old red		1			1	1
sandalwood		3			5	1
umber		3			3	1

Colours can be accurately mixed in a saucer by adding the measured water colours from a small spoon, but it is often better to let the two or three colours blend naturally on the paper.

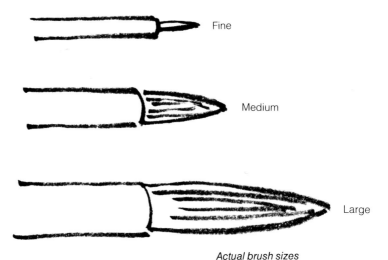

Fine

Medium

Large

Actual brush sizes

Brushes

Instructions for the paintings in this book describe the brushes needed as being either fine, medium or large. Many brushes have numbers on them, but these numbers vary from brush manufacturer to brush manufacturer. All the paintings in this book have been achieved using one of the three following sized brushes. In fact, most of the basic compositions could be painted with the medium brush only, once control of the point has been achieved. Practice will demonstrate how easy it is to use these Chinese brushes with control and variety.

Colour Uses

Young grass in spring is conveyed by greens and blues, while different combinations of these two colours produce the shades of thick summer grass. In autumn the grass withers and yellow and brown are the colours to be mixed to convey this seasonal change.

Mountain birds, living in the trees, require all five colours for their plumage. The phoenix and the pheasant have red and green feathers. Clear colours, since they are continually bathing in the flowing streams, are used for water birds, which should be painted in blues and greens – unless, like the female mandarin duck or the kingfisher, they need all five colours to convey the brilliance of their plumage.

The peacock is a favourite subject for Chinese painters

The following list indicates some traditional uses for the colours, not necessarily in their pure form, but in shades and tones as appropriate.

crimson   flowers, figures, sky
vermilion flowers, men's clothes, leaves, pagodas, temples, figures, camellia, lotus, maple, tallow tree, persimmon, chestnut
yellow   flowers, landscape, leaves in autumn, clothing, some pine tree bark, mountain slopes and paths
blue   clothes (dark), landscape (light), dotting leaves, back of paintings, flowers
white   figures
green   landscape, trees

Shades of Blue

There are two basic kinds of Chinese pigment colours – mineral and vegetable. Azurite blue is a mineral colour and indigo is a vegetable pigment.

Hydrangea on silk, painted by the author. The fan-shaped format is a very popular one. In this case the shape has been cut out in mounting card and the silk mounted behind it. The silk painting can be used as a window picture, where because the painting has no backing, light will shine through the material and the colours will have an additional glow

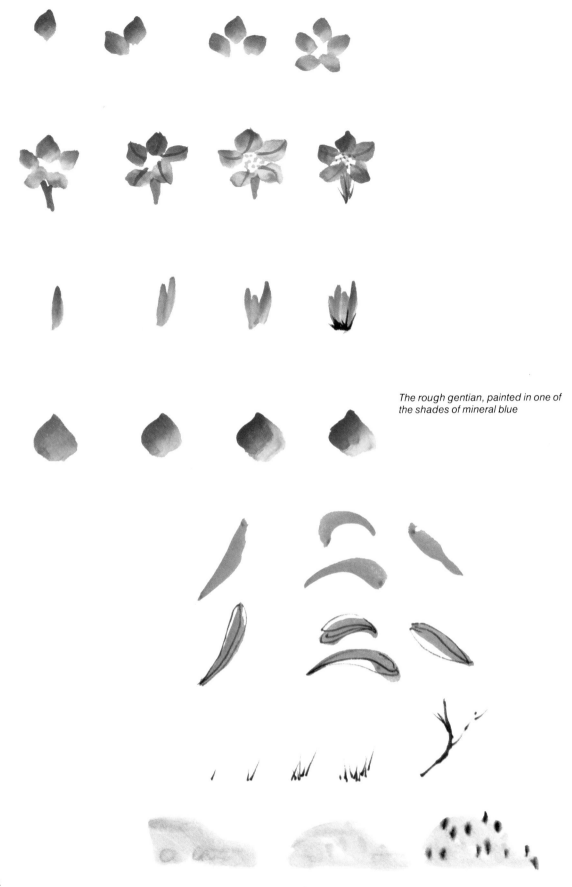

The rough gentian, painted in one of the shades of mineral blue

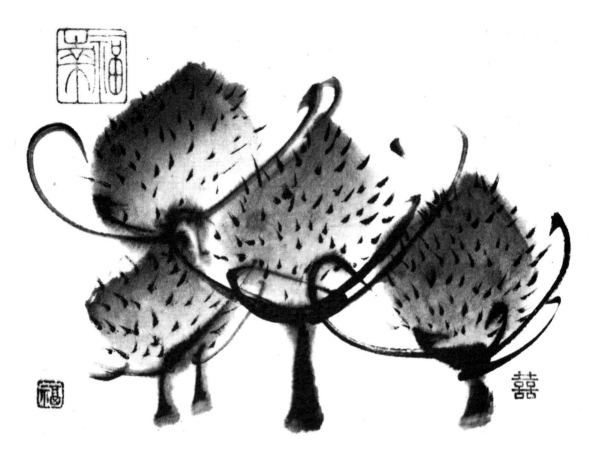

Teasel heads – indigo and browns mixed wetly and allowed to run on absorbent rice paper

Mineral Blue (sometimes called shih ch'ing, *or azurite, approx. = Ultramarine)*

It is used in three shades:

Light and clear for the faces of leaves and for landscapes;

Medium for blue flowers, for accentuating the heads and backs of birds, for dotting between leaves or for washes on the backs of paintings;

Dark for garments in figure painting, for touches on leaves and for accents on the wings and the tails of birds.

Indigo Blue (tien hua)

This is used for stronger touches on birds and flowers and for distant mountains and for outlining or the veins on leaves.

This painting of a large yellow flower demonstrates the two techniques of 'outline' and 'solid stroke'

Mixing the Blues

For flowers a touch of red can be added to the mineral blue.

Indigo can be added to green for birds such as the kingfisher.

Indigo added to greens enhances the reds and pinks of the nearby flowers and so they complement each other.

Indigo with red produces lotus green (*lien ch'ing*).

Indigo and white produce the pale green where lotus roots join.

6 parts indigo and 4 parts vegetable yellow produce old green (*Lao lu*).

3 parts indigo and 7 parts vegetable yellow produce young, fresh green (*man lu*).

'*Ch'ing ch'u yu lan*' – Chinese saying meaning, 'as green comes from blue and is superior to it'.

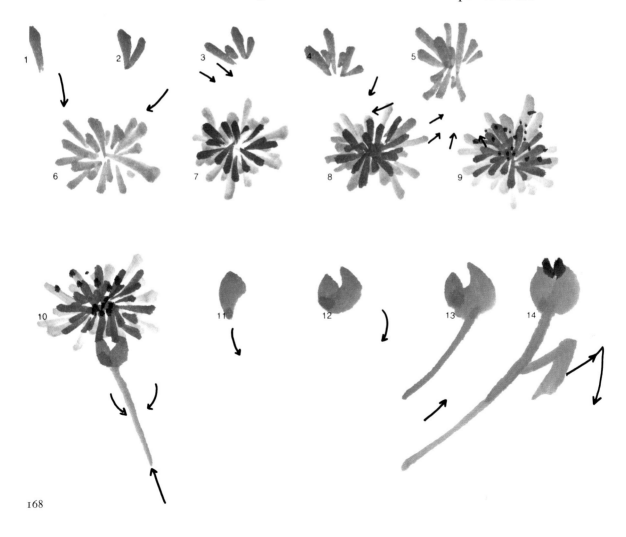

Cornflowers, painted by the author

有時三點雨兩點雨

到霎十枝五枝花

ometimes a flower painting can be enhanced by the
ddition of a piece of calligraphy, one of the most usual
orms being that of the couplet.

rom T. C. Lai's book *Chinese Couplets* a suitable one
night be:

Sometimes two or three drops of rain;
Everywhere five or ten sprigs of flowers.'

169

Blue Landscapes

There was a special kind of landscape, always painted in the blue-green style, which was called *Ch'ing lu shan shui*, but perhaps more common in modern Chinese landscape painting is the 'Indigo-style' landscape.

Indigo-style landscape

Lightly wash umber over the basic ink structure with some indigo. Then sky and water are lightly washed in with indigo. (NB, small pieces of paper can be used as a blotter to absorb any surplus or excessive colour.) Finally, the whole picture is given a delicate indigo wash. The colour, because it is transparent, serves to intensify and emphasise the original structural elements.

Hsuan-jan are small areas of wash.

Jan is the overall wash applied evenly to large areas of painting.

'Jan' can cover '*Hsuan-jan*'.

The Indigo Landscape

Colours: black, indigo, umber

Brushes: fine, medium, large

Steps: (Paint 1–8 in shades of black)

1 (Medium brush) Paint rocks in pale black to give main landscape structure.

2 Paint trees on rock Groups A and C: trunks with the medium brush and leaves with the fine brush.

3 With a fine brush, paint the fisherman between Groups A and B.

4 Medium black, dry black, add structure lines to all rock groups.

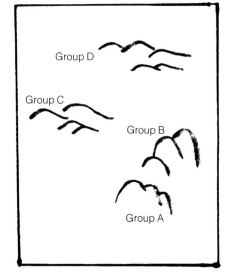

Groups of rocks labelled A–D in order of painting

Chinese fishermen

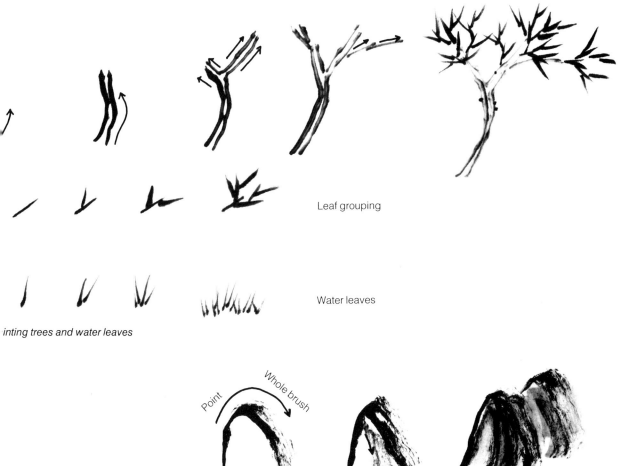

Leaf grouping

Water leaves

inting trees and water leaves

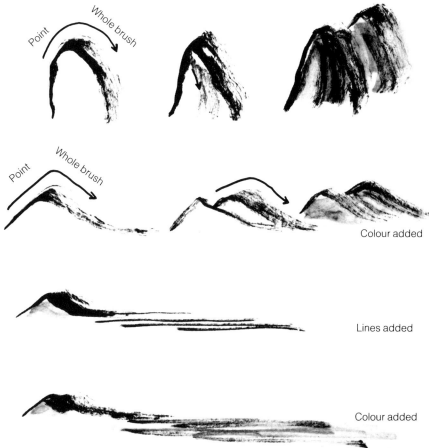

Point Whole brush

Point Whole brush

Colour added

Lines added

Colour added

How to paint the rocks and low-lying hills

5 With the fine brush loaded with black, make flick strokes for water-growing leaves and some leaves on Group D rocks.

6 With medium brush, make individual black brush strokes on Group D.

7 With medium brush, paint grey and black horizontal water lines.

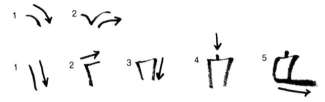

Boats and birds

8 With fine brush loaded with black, paint boats and birds. All black and grey strokes should be completed before any colour is added.

9 With medium brush, add pale indigo lines to reinforce the water lines, with some umber lines.

10 With large brush, add small wash areas to rocks in pale umber and pale indigo.

Allow painting to dry.

11 Use a large brush and, after mixing enough pale indigo, paint a wash over the whole painting, either on the front or the back of the painting.

Allow painting to dry lying flat on clean newspaper.

If suitable calligraphy is to be added to a painting, it should be completed before the addition of the all-over wash.

A suitable couplet might be:

'The azure sky mingles with the water
and the water joins with the sky –
sky and water in one colour;
The clear moon shines on the frost
and the frost reflects the moon –
moon and frost exchange brightness.'

from T.C. Lai's *Chinese Couplets*.

Calligraphic couplet for a blue landscape painting

碧天連水水連天水天一色

明月照霜霜照月月交輝

The completed blue landscape

Cornflowers (see pp. 168-9)

Colours: ultramarine, white, purple, green
Brushes: medium and fine
Steps:

1–6   Using a medium brush, mix ultramarine and white and paint individual strokes to build up the base flower.
7   With ultramarine only on the medium brush, paint a darker layer of strokes over the base flower.
8   With medium brush, add green dots to the flower centres.
9   With a fine brush, add purple dots to the centre and top of the flower.
10   With medium brush loaded with green and white mixed, paint flower base and stem.
11–13   As on diagram.
14   Add leaves and purple dots.

Paint the flowers first, then the buds, stems and finally the leaves. The stems cross each other, so the brush should not be too wet when painting them. Note that the stems are not lined up at the base.

Gentians (see pp. 164-5)

This flower originated in China and blossoms between August and September in central and north China, and between November and December in the south. It grows wild on slopes, under bushes and on the edges of forests, looking like ordinary grass until the little bell-shaped flowers burst out. It is a perennial herb with single oval leaves opposite each other. The root contains medicinal elements which are used to relieve stomach pains, fever and rheumatic problems.

Colours
Flowers: pink (scarlet + white), ultramarine blue or purple; yellow for centres; black for centres
Leaves: sky blue or green and black
Ground: brown
Brushes: medium and fine

Steps:

1 With medium brush, load brush with pink, dip point in blue and paint five-petalled star-shaped flowers. With brush point to outside of petal, paint five petals, leaving space in centre.

2 Underneath each flower paint trumpet in two strokes.

3 When flower is dry, paint pink line on each flower (fine brush).

4 (Fine brush) Add yellow dots in centre of flowers, using brush tip.

5 Paint (fine brush) black dots in flower centres when yellow is dry.

6 (Fine brush) Paint small black leaves over pink trumpet sections.

7 (Medium brush) For buds, load pink tipped with blue, three or four strokes with brush laid down on paper, tip at the top.

8 (Fine brush) Black leaves from bottom of bud and flick stroke up.

9 (Medium brush) Loaded sky blue or green mixed with small amount of black, from growing point move brush point down, along, off immediately to make rounded end.

10 (Fine brush) Add veins in black making two, three or four lines.

11 (Medium brush) Using black, make long flick strokes and one larger pushed stroke.

12 (Medium brush) Pale brown down strokes over base of stems. While wet add brush tips of yellow, followed by brush tips flat on paper of black from ink stone.

Composition:
(a) Left flower groups to be painted first, then working towards the right.
(b) Note different heights of flower groups and stems are not lined up horizontally at ground level.

Azalea with birds

Colour Harmony

Colours should be balanced so that one or two colours are stronger than the others. The dominant colour can be used sparingly, but made very striking. A subtle, light shade can be made to appear dominating by enabling it to cover a large proportion of the picture area. When talking about 'colour', several factors have to be considered. Colour consists of the pigment itself (red, yellow or blue, etc.); it embraces the concept of 'tone' (light or dark), and the saturation level (bright or dull).

Winter Jasmine is a painting which expresses some of these concepts.

Winter Jasmine

Begonia

White is the highest possible tone, while black is the lowest. White is often added to colours, therefore, to raise their tonal value (sometimes called 'tinting'), while adding black to a colour lowers its tone (referred to as 'shading').

The large unpainted areas of white paper left exposed in Chinese paintings contribute to the tonality of the result and influence the mood of the painting. Shades of black integrated into the ink washes are also examples of tonality.

Nacissus shows how this can be so effective.

Saturation of colour is its intensity or vividness and is usually not a notable feature of Chinese painting.

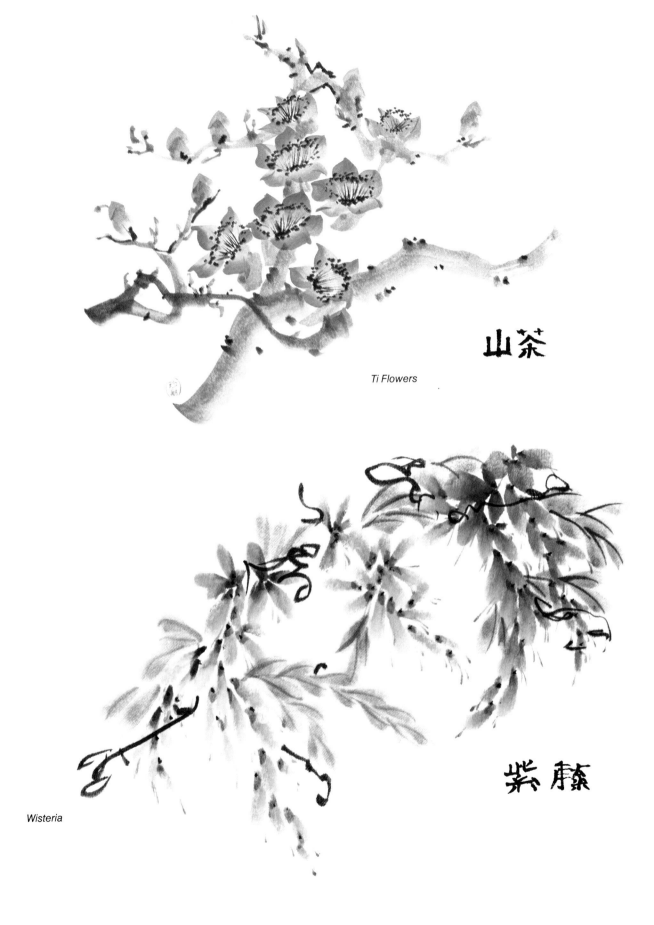

山茶

Ti Flowers

紫藤

Wisteria

Narcissus

水仙

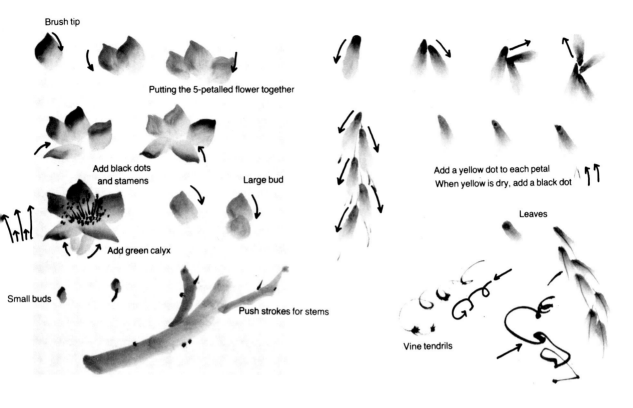

Brush tip

Putting the 5-petalled flower together

Add black dots and stamens

Large bud

Add a yellow dot to each petal
When yellow is dry, add a black dot

Leaves

Add green calyx

Small buds

Push strokes for stems

Vine tendrils

Two-colour Brush Loading

Blending two colours in the brush before making the stroke is very effective. The brush should be loaded first with the main colour and then the end dipped into a different colour. For example:

Main brush loading colour	*Tip loading colour*
(a) dilute gamboge	red ochre
(b) indigo	black ink
(c) vermilion	dark red
(d) white	crimson lake

The famous Chinese flower called 'the ti flower' shows two-colour loading at its most effective.

Three-colour Brush Loading

Colours in order:

(a) white	(b) yellow	(c) red	roses
(a) light green	(b) dark green	(c) black	leaves
(a) pink	(b) blue	(c) purple	wisteria

Outline Iris with butterfly painted on bamboo paper

Using White

The Chinese advise that a little hot water can be added to the white when it is to be used, both for the painting of white flowers and for when it is to be mixed with colours. A light coating of the white can also be added to the back of the painting to enhance its whiteness.

If white is to be used as infill colour, with black outlines, then especial care needs to be taken so that it does not run into the outlines. It is best to apply the white lightly and put on several coats. If the white is too thick and accidentally overlaps the outline so that it needs to be retouched, the effect of the whole picture will be spoiled. In general, white should be used with care, as it tends to darken with age.

When white flowers such as the lotus or the water lily are being painted, the tips of the petals can be touched up with white, which accentuates the form and gives strength to the stamens. Most white flower petals can be touched up in this way.

Some flowers, like the water lily and the hibiscus, have veins in their petals which can be traced in white and then colour added over the top. Stamens are often dotted in with white also.

In any paintings of flowers where the colours have been mixed with white, the colours will be enhanced by a coat of white on the back. If the colours are clear and light, then pure white should be used for the backing colour, but if the colours are dark or low key, then the backing white should be used only when tinted with the same colours.

Ti or Tea Flower (see pp. 181, 183)

There are nearly two hundred varieties of this bush plant, some with single petals, others with double-petalled flowers. They occur in a variety of colours from white to yellow, peach, pink, crimson and, in this case, the brilliant cinnabar red. The leaves are dark green, thick and hard and, of course, can be used for brewing tea. Many Chinese poets have written verses to this beautiful flower.

Colours: black, yellow, vermilion, green

Brush: medium

知人者智自知者明勝人者有力自勝者強

Blossom on brown rice paper
showing the white stamens with a
poem from the Tao Te Ching
which reads:

*Knowing others is wisdom
Knowing the self is enlightenment
Mastering others requires force
Mastering the self needs strength.'*

Steps:

1 Paint the main branches, leaving space for the flowers. The stroke used is a push stroke with the brush loaded in grey tipped with green.

2 Paint the flowers with the brush loaded with yellow tipped with vermilion.

3 Add the stamens and black pollen dots when the flower is dry.

4 Paint the green calyx under each flower.

5 Paint the large buds next.

6 Add smaller stems and twigs and join any flowers to stems using grey.

7 Add some black dots and small line emphases in black on the stems.

Winter Jasmine (see p. 177)

The winter jasmine is a central and northern shrub in China, growing on slopes and precipices. It is a deciduous member of the olive family with yellow flowers blooming from February to April.

Colours: yellow, black, brown
Brushes: medium and fine
Steps:

1 (Medium brush) Paint main stems in black, leaving spaces for some flower groups.
2 (Medium brush) Paint yellow flowers. Put brush down on paper, tip towards growing point to make ⌒⁊ shape.
3 (Fine brush) Do free thin brown lines to outline bud flowers. Brown dot in group to indicate flower centre.
4 (Fine brush) Thin brown stems for hanging buds and flowerless new stems.

Polyanthus Narcissus (see p. 182)

The Chinese narcissus is native to the marshy lands along the southeastern coast and is in full bloom around the end of the year. Its name from ancient days has been 'riding on the wave fairy'. It is a member of the amaryllis family with egg-shaped bulbs covered in dark brown skin. The root is white and the light green leaves are long and thick. Four to eight flowers bloom on the straight stalks.

Colours: black, yellow, green brown
Brushes: fine and medium

Hibiscus – pink flowers with white vein lines

Steps:

1 With the fine brush paint the black outlines of the six-petalled flowers and buds.

2 Paint the black outlines of the leaves with the fine brush.

3 Next paint the stems in black with the same brush.

4 With a medium brush add the black dots in the flower heads and the thick strokes at the base of the leaves.

5 A medium brush loaded in yellow provides the centres.

6 Mixing yellow and green on the medium brush, or brown and green, or all three, paint pale washes on the leaves and flower stems and in the centre of the flowers.

Wisteria (see pp. 181, 183)

Colours: pink, blue, purple, yellow, green, black
Brushes: medium and fine
Steps:

1 With a medium brush, paint the flowers by putting the whole brush down on to the paper, having loaded in three colours. To do this, load the brush first with pink, then scrape off two thirds, load this two thirds with blue then scrape off one third and load the tip of the bristles with purple.

2 When dry, add yellow dots with a medium brush.

3 With the medium brush add black dots on top of the yellow.

4 With the fine brush add the flowers' hanging stems in purple.

5 Using the medium brush again, paint the leaves in medium green.

6 Central leaf veins are added in dark green with the fine brush.

7 The black-loaded fine brush is needed to add the tendrils to enhance the composition. The stroke should be continuous in flow, but may leave the paper.

It is not possible to join Chinese strokes together exactly if the brush leaves the paper. It is better to leave a space. The Chinese say: 'Brush absent, spirit present.'

Colour Pigments and Painting Surfaces

A little colour pigment mixed with water produces a transparent solution, while adding more pigment makes the solution more opaque. The mineral pigments are deeper and richer in colour than the vegetable pigments.

A very important constituent in Chinese painting is the glue, which not only binds the pigment together, but acts as a fixative for the colour as it dries. Colours or inks, therefore, can be painted on top of each other without causing any running or bleeding. The fixative also helps to bond the pigment into the paper so that it does not run when washes are added or paste is used for the mounting process. When raw silk is used as the painting surface, the pigment sinks into the surface, diluting the colour and impairing the quality of the line. To deal with this problem, silk used to be treated with size, which made the material less absorbent, but the only way to paint on it was to use slow, careful movements, resulting in rather formal compositions. Spontaneous brushwork is at its most effective on absorbent paper which sucks the pigment from the brush. Chinese paper, with its long fibres, does not disintegrate when wet, but the amount of water taken in is difficult to manage. Papers, therefore, are sized to produce different degrees of absorbency. Sizing makes the paper smoother and the surface slightly water-resistant.

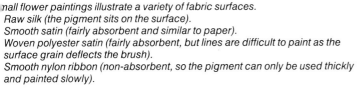

nall flower paintings illustrate a variety of fabric surfaces.
Raw silk (the pigment sits on the surface).
Smooth satin (fairly absorbent and similar to paper).
Woven polyester satin (fairly absorbent, but lines are difficult to paint as the surface grain deflects the brush).
Smooth nylon ribbon (non-absorbent, so the pigment can only be used thickly and painted slowly).

he texture of silk is regular and porous as created by the
arp and weft. Sized paper has a tighter texture and,
though it seems smooth, there are subtle variations
roduced by its base vegetable-type content and the way
which it was dried. Brush strokes themselves have a
xture according to the amount of liquid in the brush.
he combination of dry and wet brush strokes on different
ualities of sized papers produces a variety of textural
fects. Sometimes individual brush movements leave
eir traces on the paper, other times the brush is wiped
cross the surface, magnifying the effect on paper with a
inimally sized surface.

e results of adding water to the pigment.
ark green has been used as the base pigment. The first four leaf strokes have
d progressively more water added, while the horizontal fifth stroke is a result of
dding white pigment to the green. The first four shades demonstrate how the
gment becomes more and more transparent, although the weaker, wetter
lour is much more difficult to handle. However, it is not an acceptable
ernative to add white, which produces a paler, but non-transparent colour.

e two red pigments are: cinnabar red, which is a vegetable colour, and blood
d, which is a mineral colour. The mineral blood red is deeper and richer than the
getable cinnabar.

A vertical dry brush stroke and a leaf stroke on four different papers.
1 Ordinary white rice paper (great absorbency).
2 Bamboo paper (slightly brown in colour; smooth but not very absorbent).
3 A white coarse-fibred paper (absorbent, but the brush flow is interrupted by the fibres).
4 A lightly dyed paper with positive vertical grain (medium absorbency).

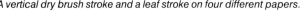

Most painting surfaces have a smooth and a rough side which can be gauged by touch. Painting is usually carried out on the smooth side unless a special effect is required. Care should always be taken not to drag the brush with too much pressure over the painting surface, particularly in the case of paper, as this may scrape the surface off.

Painting Surfaces

The painting surface is vitally important for Chinese techniques as it influences the style which may be used for the best results. Whether the surface is rough or smooth, dull or glossy, or more or less absorbent considerably affects the way in which the ink or colour leaves the brush to combine with the surface. Basically there are two different styles of painting: the careful and the more spontaneous free-style.

Flower painting by Mary Howard,
one of the author's students

The careful style reflects the more academic type of painting and is called *kung pi* which means 'industrious' or 'labouring' brush. In essence it is almost like drawing. The brush, which is held vertically with only the tip touching the surface, is used to produce lines. *Kung pi* requires a less absorbent surface to keep the lines clean and clear, so sized paper or sized silk is the easiest surface on which to paint.

The free, spontaneous style, which can produce 'flying white' or 'splashed ink' paintings, uses the brush in a slanting manner, where absorbency is the key to the exuberant results. The brush needs to open out on the paper, so unsized papers or rough silks with the same characteristics are required for the surface material on which to paint. This is the style of the non-academic painters, the monks and scholars of the Southern School of painters who prefer to paint solely in shades of black.

In the spontaneous style, over-painting does not usually occur, so each brush stroke is of vital importance, while paintings in the careful style, where colour is added mainly as a fill-in, can have some controlled line additions made if necessary.

Landscape painting by Doug Wells, one of the author's students

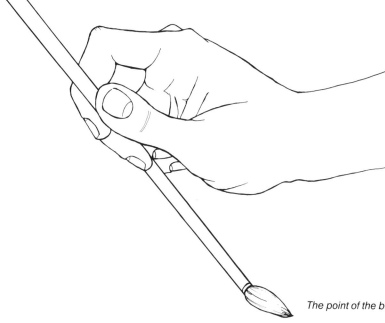

The point of the brush leads the stroke direction

Paper

Many of the various types of paper bear poetic names, such as the Sung paper called 'Paper from the Pure Heart Hall', bamboo pulp paper called *hsüan chih*, which is white and fine and still in use either sized or unsized, old treasure house roll called *chiu k'u p'i* and the mirror-smooth paper called *ching mien kuang*. In the main these can be divided into two categories: the more absorbent, unsized papers and the less absorbent, sized ones.

Unsized papers, being most suitable for the spontaneous type of brushwork, are usually dominated by free ink strokes which run easily on the paper, so good control is essential, particularly as each kind of paper has a different degree of absorbency. All unsized papers dry slowly, as the surface is quite rough. Ink and light colours only are accomplished best on these papers and although the brush strokes are quickly completed individually, the painting can take quite a long time to finish because of the paper's slow drying qualities.

Nowadays, sized papers can be purchased ready for painting, although some artists still prepare their own. Animal or fish-bone glue is mixed with size made of alum and then painted on to the paper so that it is thoroughly soaked. The side on which the mixture has been applied is smoother than the other side and is usually the one used for painting.

In addition to the actual effect of the glue and size, the fact that this paper has already been thoroughly wetted means that some of the absorbent qualities have been already used up, so that the ink or colour will not run so quickly and the sized paper will dry much more quickly than the unsized paper.

Of course, the very experienced painter is capable of producing either free or linear strokes on both sized and unsized paper, but, in general, using the most appropriate surface produces the best results.

Frog and flowers painted on Japanese Ganpishi paper. Notice that the flower leaves have broken edges and the strokes for the water plants allow both water run and pigment collection

Chinese vegetables are a very popular subject for Chinese paintings and in particular the Chinese cabbage (or Chinese leaves)

Silk

As a painting surface, it is necessary to size silk before it can be used at all, otherwise the paint has no adhesion and runs right through the material. The closeness of the weave also affects its qualities as a painting surface, but, in general, its characteristic behaviour when used for Chinese painting is somewhere between sized and unsized paper.

Because the silk is sized it dries quickly and gives sharply defined strokes when the amount of liquid in the brush is carefully controlled. However, because of the material's weave, the surface is not as smooth as sized paper, so that it also takes the free brush relatively well.

Most Chinese artists tend to use silk more for colour-based paintings than for those where black is the dominant medium. Moreover, because silk does not need to be back mounted, the colours used are often stronger than if paper was the painting surface. Examples of the same composition painted on different surfaces demonstrate the

Iris and rock painted by the author on coloured rice paper. It is possible, although difficult, to obtain dyed Chinese paper, but due to the dye having used up most of the paper's absorbent qualities, the surface reacts to the brush in a non-absorbent manner

Begonia. Notice the texture of the vein lines on the leaves which have been affected by the grain of the silk when the strokes are painted in different directions

This angel fish by Mabel Daniels has been painted on a type of card. The pigment tends to 'sit' on the surface when the painting surface has little or no absorbency

important part that paper and silk play in conveying style and mood in Chinese paintings.

In *The Way of the Brush*, Van Briessen describes Chinese painting as 'endless philosophising with a brush, an instinctive worship of one of the central ideas of the Chinese mind – that of Yin and Yang, the opposites which are complementary, the interplay of masculine and feminine'.

Yang (masculine)	Yin (feminine)
brush	paper
using the brush	using the ink
sized paper (hard)	unsized paper (soft)
sized paper	unsized paper
strong brushwork	easier brushwork

Colour Washes

A wash is achieved when the pigment is spread in large areas over the surface of the paper so that the individual brush strokes are not generally apparent. Large, soft brushes are needed for big areas of wash, with the brush held at an angle to allow more bristles to sweep across the surface area.

There are five possible methods of applying a wash to a Chinese painting.

1 After painting in the ink contours first, the colour wash should be added inside the lines. This is used mainly with the outline flower technique.

Mix the colour with water in a saucer and use the brush to stir together. To obtain the right shade, add either more water or more colour. If large amounts of this type of wash are needed, all exactly the same shade, then ensure that a sufficient quantity is prepared. However, it is often better to mix small amounts for flower painting so that each flower is a slightly different colour and the picture becomes more varied.

2 For larger areas, such as water or sky, the wash is again applied after all the black–ink painting is finished, but this time the paper can first be wetted with clean water (the excess moisture being removed by dabbing with another piece of absorbent paper) and then the colour applied. It occasionally helps to have another *clean* brush ready to smooth in the painting strokes, which should all have been applied in the same direction.

It is not essential to wet the paper first before applying the wash. The slightly 'cockled' effect as the paper dries will disappear if the completed dry painting is flattened under a weight such as a heavy book.

If traces of the brush show when painting water, it is called *tzu* (saturating), while the light ink and dry brush wash used for waterfalls is called *fen* (dividing).

It is quite permissible to apply several layers of wash, each time waiting until the previous wash is thoroughly dry. Very interesting colour effects can be obtained using this method.

Snowy Landscape. As areas of the painting have to be left blank to indicate the snow, this silk painting has had to have its areas of wash applied very carefully

Poppies. The flowers' petals have been infilled with small areas of wash

Village Palms. A small silk landscape with a pink all-over wash

Fu Baoishi (1904-1965) used to accomplish his translucent washes by painting them with a dry brush on wet paper in his studio. Sitting by the fire, drinking wine, he found that the heat of the fire dried the paper very quickly, making the wash paler than usual.

Three or four layers of light ink washes are called *hsuan* – meaning wash. Soaking the whole painting is called *hua* – meaning cleansing.

3 Another technique which can be employed to obtain a smooth all-over wash is to apply the colour to the reverse of the painting. Most Chinese paper has a

*A Chinese Landscape.
This painting was given an
all-over wash with tea
to produce a fine even
antique tone*

smooth side and a rough side. It is usual to paint on the
smooth side of the paper, so that the brush strokes will
flow more easily over the surface. However, for an
overall one-colour wash, normally applied in a pale tone
after the main body of the painting is finished, the paint
may be applied either on the right side or the 'wrong'
side of the paper.

4 To create an impression of antiquity, some painters use
tea as the wash medium. Testing on small samples of
the painting surface first, to see what strength of 'brew'
is required, a suitable colour can be applied to any

Black Swans. Two versions of the same painting, demonstrating the effect of a crackle wash

painting, whether on silk or paper. It is most effective when used on white paper, and landscapes benefit greatly from this type of wash.

5 Crackle wash is a rather unusual modern type of applied background, to be used on paper only. It developed from the ancient technique of Batik. When the compositional element of the painting is completely finished and thoroughly dry, the area to be crackled is crumpled up in the hand and pressed firmly so that creases appear. In the first instance this should be tried experimentally with a whole small painting and definitely not with 'a masterpiece'. Then open out the painting so that it is reasonably flat, but do not press too hard as it is vital to retain the creases as raised areas. The wash is then applied with a not too saturated brush, loading the brush so that it is not as wet as it would be for a normal wash. The brush should pass gently over the paper with little pressure. The raised sections will absorb the water, leaving the hollows or cracks untouched. A random pattern of colour and untouched paper will result which very effectively represents water or undelineated green foliage. Light colours, blues and greens, are most suitable for crackle wash.

Possible Faults and Solutions

Fault
(a) The original painted colours, under the wash, run.
(i)   *Reason* The original colours were put on too quickly.
      To avoid this Use less pigment in the original painting.
OR
(ii) *Reason* The basic painting was not dry when the wash was applied.
      To avoid this Allow the basic composition to dry thoroughly before applying the wash.
(b) Uneven patches appear in the wash.
(i)   *Reason* Not enough paint was mixed for the wash and more had to be made quickly.
      To avoid this Mix more wash than you think will be sufficient. The paper absorbs a great deal.
OR
(ii) *Reason* The wash brush was applied in different directions.
      To avoid this Apply the wash horizontally from left to right.

OR

(iii) *Reason* The wash dried too rapidly.

To avoid this Allow the painting to dry slowly, laid flat on an absorbent surface such as newspaper or blotting paper.

OR

(iv) *Reason* The brush strokes overlapped when the wash was applied.

To avoid this Apply all the large, soft hairs of the brush to the paper in regular strokes.

(c) White spaces appear where they were not intended to be.

(i) *Reason* The brush strokes were not applied evenly.

To avoid this Apply the wash brush to the paper in regular strokes.

Depending upon the composition, it may give an added dimension to the painting if some areas are of stronger colour due to two layers of pigment overlapping, or it may be beneficial to the painting if streaks of the white base paper are allowed to show.

(d) The painting paper tears.

(i) *Reason* Too much brush pressure has been applied.

To avoid this Let the brush glide smoothly over the paper without pressing too hard.

(e) Scraped surface – bits of the paper collect in small lumps.

(i) *Reason* Too much pressure has been applied to the paper surface.

To avoid this Be much gentler with the wash brush and ensure that the brush is not too dry.

(f) Blotches of paint appear in the wash.

(i) *Reason* The material underneath the painting paper is not absorbent enough and liquid goes through the Chinese paper and is then pushed back into the painting.

To avoid this Use more absorbent material underneath the painting.

OR

(ii) *Reason* The brush did not move continuously across the paper, but paused *en route*.

To avoid this Make the even brush movements essential for a smooth wash.

The boats and the tiny birds help balance the composition in this landscape

The Elements of Chinese Composition

Even when painting a natural scene, the artist involves himself or herself in both conscious and unconscious choices. In Chinese painting in particular, where the choice of painting subject evolves from the mind and not by sitting, sketch book in hand, looking at a flower, animal, insect or scene, the artist's own memory, mood or predilection forms the general composition before brush touches paper. Composition is a crucial element in this conceptual form of art, which is also endeavouring to convey a philosophy of nature through painting. Chinese painting is a studio art. The painter sits alone reflecting on his memories, shaping the natural external world to fit his own emotional concepts. The principles of Chinese composition are based upon the ebb and flow of opposite strands which relate to each other, like gossamer threads, woven across the painting in a complicated intertwining pattern. The Chinese call these 'connections' dragon veins (*lung mo*). It is simplest to understand when watching an artist paint. The addition of a small dot, another branch, a boat in the distance, can suddenly make the painting come alive, as though the overall balance of the composition has suddenly been completed.

The Host–Guest principle (*pin chu*), where an element of the composition is set in a paired relationship representing the passive and aggressive, is common to most Chinese paintings. The best examples are shown in three groupings, where two trees stand side by side, one bending towards or enfolding the other. Usually the trees are contrasting in types or, alternatively, one is thin and straight, while the other is of different height and width. Parallel lines and clumsy curves are avoided. Sometimes the pair is described as 'taking each other's hands' as branches intertwine in friendly proximity. The principle is then expanded in the composition to include another group of trees which bears a Host–Guest relationship to the first pair.

Trees, taking each other's hands

Compositions include not just trees, but mountains, rocks and people, related in this way. Moreover, it is not sufficient merely for parts of a composition to be related, it is also necessary for the entire painting to be combined to form a cohesive whole.

This extension of the Host–Guest principle is called 'Opening and Closing' (*k'ai ho*). Where short threads hold the small elements together, long threads hold the entire picture together.

Some elements open up the picture, opposing elements give it stability, completing a painting by turning towards each other, while at the same time forming a contrast. These pictures illustrate some of the different ways in which this principle is applied. Of course, the focus of a painting never occurs in the middle of the painting area, otherwise the composition would appear totally static.

Chinese artists place great emphasis on capturing the illusion of nature in an impressionistic manner. Paintings cannot be truly abstract, but have to have recognisable subject matter. This was laid down as one of the six important rules of Chinese painting by Hsieh Ho in the fifth century AD.

The dictionary defines perspective as 'the art of drawing objects on a surface so as to give the effect of distance, solidity etc.' It is the way in which a painter can make it appear that the viewer looks through nearer distance towards things in the far distance. The Chinese painter employs two general techniques to achieve this. Linear perspective, which involves proportion and placing; and atmospheric perspective, which depends upon the use of clear tone and colour.

'Up' is the far distance in landscape paintings, usually arranged on a diagonal, often following the meanderings of a river.

Another method used to denote far and near is demonstrated by dividing the landscape into three distinct sections to represent near, middle and far distance. This is an artistic multiple vision not in any way realistic, as the eye could not possibly take in at one look all the elements of the panorama spread out to the view.

*One pair of opening and
closing elements*

Atmospheric perspective, where far distant areas are paler
in colour and tone, is generally demonstrated by
mountains shrouded in mist or rocks and trees with
unclear lines. Voids, the unmarked area of paper which the
brush has not touched, also serve to render by means of
the blank space the size and distance of a landscape
painting.

Ancient Chinese beliefs about the relationship of Heaven
to Earth are also reflected in the painting composition.
This principle (*t'ien ti*) concerns the disposition of the
upper and lower areas so that they relate to the each other
in harmony, thus achieving a vertical balance.

At the moment when the first brush stroke touches the
paper, all these compositional elements have been
considered, perhaps not consciously, but because years of
practice have infiltrated the mind's consciousness. It is the
Chinese aspects of composition which prove most difficult
to the Westerner attempting traditional painting.

To emulate the Chinese painters, it is necessary to work through the same disciplines of practice and copying from the Masters which they undertook, which will, in time, produce an instinctive knowledge of how a composition should be formed.

The painting builds itself up from the first brush stroke; a single leaf becomes a group, a tree becomes a forest, then all combine to produce a pleasing entity.

The principles of Host and Guest, Opening and Closing, Heaven and Earth are evident at each stage of the painting, continuously developing towards the final result.

Three examples of paintings with two or more pairs of opening-closing elements in each

*A landscape with three distinct
sections to give perspective*

*Voids of space to give atmosphere
are elements of this landscape*

The harmony of vertical balance

This flower and butterfly painting
embodies all the previous principles
to make a cohesive entity

Chinese Gardens

A Chinese garden represents the symbolic essence of nature. Here the painter can sit or stroll, watching and absorbing the 'nature of nature'. Such gardens are not filled with a plethora of flowers and shrubs, or distinguished by vistas of grassy swards. They are not formal, symmetrical arrangements, but carefully conceived areas of nature in harmony, replicating in miniature the vastness of the universal landscape. Poetry, calligraphy, landscape painting and gardening are interwoven arts, not all to be taken in at once, but to be discovered bit by bit from ever-changing viewpoints. Plants are not the most important elements of a Chinese garden: it combines rocks, water, trees, white walls and pavilions in such a way that small spaces expand mysteriously as the seasons change. Courtyards, like space-cells, merge from one to another, leading the visitor into small havens of different experiences. From different viewpoints the enclosed privacy expands as branches move in the wind against the white lattice walls, leading the eye into the distance, hazily seen through a decorative archway.

Nature in Harmony

The Chinese Garden

The Chinese garden is a celebration of change. Peonies grown together in one garden area might be the focus in early summer when visitors would arrive to honour them by party-like enjoyment, sitting sipping wine, writing poetry and enjoying the view. As the summer heat increased the garden guests would move to a cooler area, possibly an open pavilion (called a *t'ing*) set near the water, where water lilies could be admired in their natural setting.

Autumn was a time to appreciate chrysanthemums or orchids. Houses without gardens would make their gardens in pots. Large bowls filled with lotus might stand in the courtyard or either side of the main entrance, to be changed for chrysanthemums as the season moved on. Herbaceous plants, dwarf trees and miniature landscapes were also possible for those without much space. Even fish could swim lazily in the large open-mouthed Chinese jars made specially for the purpose. Indeed, fish were bred specifically to be seen and appreciated from above.

The essence of a Chinese garden may lie more in the calm, ever-changing delights which appear throughout the seasons than in the actual flowers and trees themselves.

Owners gave their gardens evocative names such as Dreamy Tower, the Place of Clear Meditation, the Bower of Nature, or they referred specifically to special garden

Sipping wine in the garden (from The Mustard Seed Garden)

Waterside Garden

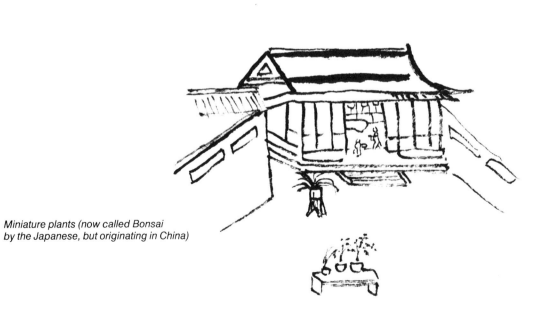

*Miniature plants (now called Bonsai
by the Japanese, but originating in China)*

Fish swimming among the lotus

features – the Plum Slope, the Lotus Cove, the Peach Tree Banks. The Chinese poet Yuan Mei in the 1750s was said to have had a garden with twenty-four separate named pavilions. '*Cho Cheng Yuan*', a garden in Soochow, means 'Garden of the Unsuccessful Politician'.

A very ancient game, celebrated in many paintings and poems, was exemplified by the eighteenth-century Peking 'Pavilion of the Floating Cups'. The pavilion, standing over a stream in the garden, was used by guests, who had to compose a poem in the time it took a wine-cup to float down the channel of water from one end to the other. Failure meant drinking the wine and trying again. Many famous poems were written in these circumstances!

Characteristic features of a Chinese garden were the varied rocks, which represented the mountainous elements of the landscape, transferred to the smaller scale of the garden. Large standing stones, flaring out from narrow bases, hollowed by weather and time and riddled with holes, symbolised the Tao and the mountains. These stones were brought at great expense from distant areas to grace the Chinese garden. Although they are almost like sculptures, they had to be naturally formed.

Mi Fei (twelfth century) was not only a painter, poet and calligrapher, but was also noted for his love of these big stones. It is said that he bowed every day to the giant rock in his garden and called it 'elder brother'.

Horizontal Garden Landscape (painted on silk)

Landscape. Wang Wei. 11 × 14½ inches (28 × 37cm). Ink and colours on silk. The pine and the rocks are very finely drawn

The T'ang poets added a new concept to the garden – poetry carved on stone came to be regarded as essential for the enjoyment of this Chinese microcosm of life.

Two kinds of writing are found in gardens in addition to the formally inscribed couplets. There are also poems written by visitors to commemorate their enjoyment of the garden or the gatherings of friends; and the third category is the poetic names given to the different aspects of the garden, like the 'Centipede Bridge'. Later, stone walls and little bridges added shades of white and grey to the green domination of the garden.

Wang Wei (AD 699-761), the great poet-painter, is credited with the invention of the long handscroll, which, as it unrolls from right to left, connects the painted spaces by water and mist. The landscape or garden scenes roll by as the scroll is unwound, so that movement is generated from the static painting. In the same way, the small space-cells of a Chinese garden, divided by white walls representing mist, replicate the three-dimensional walk through a landscape scroll.

Ch'iu Ying (1510-1551) was a famous painter of gardens who emphasised the contrast between the 'wide-open' and the 'screened' aspects of Chinese gardens. Balustrades can have 'cracked-ice' patterns, pathways meander like playing cats, the water is a place where 'the moon washes its soul', while even buildings are constructed in shapes such as fans, plum blossoms or butterflies.

Lady meditating by a lake.
Ch'in Ying

Index